PALE ALE

The Classic Beer Style Series is devoted to offering in-depth information on world-class styles by exploring their history, flavor profiles, brewing methods, recipes, and ingredients.

PALE ALE

History, Brewing
Techniques, Recipes

Second Edition

Terry Foster

Classic Beer Style
Series No. 16

Brewers Publications
Boulder, Colorado

Brewers Publications, Division of the Association of Brewers
PO Box 1679, Boulder, CO 80306-1679
(303) 447-0816; Fax (303) 447-2825
bp@aob.org; http://beertown.org/bp

Direct all inquiries to the above address.

Printed in the United States of America
10 9 8 7 6 5 4 3 2 1

ISBN 0-937381-69-1

Please direct all inquiries to the above address.

Library of Congress Cataloging-in-Publication Data
Foster, Terry.
    Pale ale : history, brewing techniques, recipes / Terry Foster. —
Second ed.
        p.   cm. — (Classic beer style series ; 16)
    Includes bibliographical references and index.
    ISBN 0-937381-69-1 (alk. paper)
    1. Ale. I. Title. II. Series.
TP578.F67   1999
641.8'73—dc21   98-43603
                                                     CIP

This book can be dedicated only to my family. My wife, the most important person in my life, who has put up with the demands of a career requiring extensive travel, only to have me come home and either disappear downstairs to brew or upstairs to write about brewing. My son, in the hope that he will one day realize his aspirations to be a writer. My daughter, in the hope that she will one day realize how smart she really is. And last but not least, the grandchild who will be born just about the day this book is published.

Contents

Acknowledgments

There is not space enough to acknowledge all those who contributed to this book, most of them unwittingly, as I ploughed their minds and/or their writings. I suppose that most of all, I am indebted to the whole new brewing community, both amateur and professional. Its members have willingly expanded and disseminated their knowledge of beer and good brewing, with the aim of improving the quality and range of American beers. One of the great disappointments in our age of improved and improving methods of communication has been the steady dumbing down of our media, reducing everything to sound bytes and fleeting snapshots. All the more credit, then, goes to the beer writers and microbrewers who have been ready to tackle and explain the vast technical complexities of the brewing process.

If I have to name names, then I would like to thank Charlie Papazian (who got me into this Classic Beer Style Series in the first place). Charlie has done as much as anybody to popularize homebrewing.

Many other brewers and writers contributed, and I try to recognize them by citing them in the references. Stephen

Acknowledgments

Young's of southwest London is one of the proudest and fiercest defenders of real ale.

Mallery, publisher of *Brewing Techniques*, warrants mention as one who has taken the high ground in looking at the fundamentals and practicalities of brewing. And Michael Jackson will always have a place among the brewing immortals in his never-ending search for the perfect beer. Dr. John Harrison and his companions at the Durden Park Beer Circle must be commended for their extensive research into old beers and for their clear understanding that those beers must be interpreted in the eyes of the brewers and drinkers of past centuries, and not in a modern context.

Acknowledgments

Among English brewers I must thank Young's of Wandsworth, which brewed the first beer I ever drank. I thank it not just for that, but for its unswerving loyalty to real ale and its commitment to producing what it knows to be quality beer and not being pulled away from its aim to follow fashionable trends. My thanks also to David Crease for his insights on the English brewing scene and for helping to keep me sane in what sometimes seems to be a hostile world.

And of course, thanks to my publisher at Brewers Publications, Toni Knapp. Her timing was impeccable. She asked me to do this just as I was looking at a mountain of collected information and wondering what sort of book I should write next. In gratitude, I actually got the manuscript to her just before the deadline. I am afraid she will find me less compliant as we finish the details of editing!

Finally, praise and thanks to Theresa Duggan who did such a good job of making sense of not only the original but also the scrawled corrections as we went along. Her diplomacy in my struggles with the copy editor was amazing, and her ability to push everything through on time was astounding. Thank you, Theresa.

Introduction

Since I wrote the first edition of *Pale Ale*, the beer scene in both America and England has continued to ferment. Microbreweries and brewpubs have sprung up at enormous speed in both countries, and there now are more breweries in America than in Germany. On both sides of the Atlantic, the big brewing companies have acknowledged the importance of offering niche beers that have flavor by getting into the act, either by setting up their own brewpubs and micros or by buying into existing micros. Yet there is much evolution still happening, and to come.

In Britain, the laws have changed to limit the number of pubs a brewer can own. Some of the major brewers and a few of the smaller ones have gotten out of brewing entirely and simply become pub owners. Groups of independent pub-owning companies have sprung up. Using their buying power to obtain large discounts from beer suppliers, they have decreased the number of outlets available to small brewers. The result has been a reduction in choice for the customer in many cases. Now almost 30 years old, the Campaign for Real Ale (CAMRA), despite its past successes, still has much to do to ensure the survival of real draught ale.

Many English pubs have become restaurants rather than drinking places offering food on the side. Once convivial establishments have been "themed" into pseudo-Irish or American nonentities. Real ale consumption has dwindled to a relatively small part of the total beer drunk.

Conversely, most American brewpubs are restaurants, not pubs. Although they might brew good beer, beer is still a sideline to food. The last year or so has seen a

Home to Atlantic Amber Ale, New England Brewing Company is a fine new version of brewing architecture in Norwalk, Connecticut.

decline in the growth of small breweries in America and a consolidation of some of them. This might merely reflect a trend toward a more professional approach to the running of the microbrewing industry. Yet, there is still a long way to go. There are far too many bars and restaurants that offer only industrial beers.

However, unlike when I first came to America, we can now get good American-brewed beer. We just cannot always get it when or where we want it. The day when there is a "local" pub within walking distance of most drinkers is still far ahead.

Top-fermented beers and ales are still the poor cousins of lager beers. Apart from the German regional specialties of *kölsch* and *altbier*, these beers are only brewed on any scale in Britain and America. And of course, pale ale and its more popular derivative, bitter, are the main representatives of this class of beer. In the United Kingdom, pale ale is under threat from brewers who have been pushing the bland nitrogen-dispensed "smooth" ales, at the expense of the real ale that is more variable but possesses more character. The same approach is beginning to surface in America. However, American micros are generally to be commended for their return to traditional values in pale ale brewing, particularly regarding their approach to producing beers of high hop bitterness and character.

This book is an attempt to foster interest in one of the world's great beer styles and to encourage you to brew it and drink it. It is not simply a new edition of the earlier *Pale Ale*. I was pleased and honored to be asked to do that first book in the Classic Beer Style Series and even more pleased to see the way that other authors built on my humble start. After writing that book, I continued to collect historical and modern materials on pale ales, as well as other beers, and was preparing to write a book based on those materials. I was not quite sure how I was going to approach this. Toni Knapp of Brewers Publications solved the problem by approaching me and asking me to redo *Pale Ale*.

I determined that I would not simply revise the earlier book but would write a new book from the ground up. Of course, some of the material in the first book is included, but in a much-expanded form. This time, I have included a host of references for those of you who want to know more about this style of beer. Much more discussion of bitter ales has been added, since these form the largest class of pale ale derivatives in England. The chapter on dispense and real ale is considerably more comprehensive and not just limited to the narrow scope of "beer from the wood," although that is not ignored. I also include a range of new recipes. I have placed more emphasis on extract recipes, since I feel I down-played that important aspect of homebrewing in the first edition. Perhaps the biggest change is the emphasis on beers of this style that are now widely available in America.

The historical section, too, has been much expanded. Ironically, it was written in Australia, which is one of the younger countries of the world in terms of when it was settled by Europeans. Other parts were written in such places as Ukraine and Romania, areas that were settled in Roman times. I am not quite sure what that indicates about a beer style that is clearly English in origin. I suppose where it was written does not really matter, as long as you enjoy the book and find it informative. This has been a much more ambitious project than the original, and I hope I have not fallen too far short of achieving that ambition.

CHAPTER 1

The Evolution of Pale Ale

The English writer L. P. Hartley opened his novel *The Go-between* by saying, "The past is a foreign country. They do things differently there." We all too often misunderstand history by imposing today's standards and values on the past, reading modern motives and meanings into scraps of historical information. So defining a beer style on the basis of its history is an invitation to error.

Yet to ignore the history of one of the world's major classes of beer, in this case pale ale, is a fundamental mistake, if you really care about beer. This is why so many of today's factory beers are dull and tasteless, even though the brewers might still pay lip service to the style. We often also forget that history is not just about dead things and people; it still lives, and today will be history tomorrow.

This is especially true regarding India pale ale (IPA), *the* original English pale ale style. Over the last 200 years, English IPAs (or at least those beers designated as such by their brewers) have become watered-down travesties of their nineteenth-century forebears. In contrast, modern American microbrewers and pub brewers have, in their new IPAs, returned to the style's roots, restoring it to something close to its former glories. However, relatively little recipe data is available for re-creating any beer of earlier centuries. A 1990 survey by England's Manchester University showed that of 620 English breweries, only 70 had pre-1914 brew house data. There are published recipes from the eighteenth and nineteenth centuries. However, the limited access to actual brewing books means these recipes might not be representative of common practice.[1]

But I am getting ahead of myself. The origins of pale ale are quite murky (as probably were the early versions of the ale itself!). Ale in its original sense was beer before the arrival of hops, an event that occurred perhaps as early as the eighth century in Europe, but not until the fifteenth century in England. Hops were introduced to England by Dutch and Flemish immigrants who settled in London on the South Bank of the Thames. Southwark (the area just below London Bridge) became the trading area for hops. Many merchants set up there, handling the hops that initially were grown in Kent and other areas of the South. Ultimately, a building dedicated to this market was erected. Called, not surprisingly, the Hop Exchange, it still exists just a few hundred yards from London Bridge, behind the Borough Market, although it no longer handles the produce for which it is named. Its interior is very attractive, with galleries encircling an atrium, each faced in wrought iron in which the twin motifs of hop flowers and the Kentish County white horse symbol embrace. Appropriately, just around the corner from the Hop Exchange is a microbrewery, Bishops, whose beers are some of the hoppiest and bitterest you can hope to find.

The main entrance to the Hop Exchange in Southwark. Located close to the London Bridge, the Hop Exchange was in operation for less than two years.

Ale was not hopped, although many other herbs were often used to flavor it. Beer, on the other hand, was hopped ale, and it was not at first readily accepted by the English drinker, being regarded by many as a curious import. Many stories exist about this antipathy to hops, including that of Henry VIII's banning his own brewer from using them.[2] But hops had a great advantage over other flavorings in that their bitterness was the perfect balance for the cloying sweetness of the strong ales of the time, so much so that eventually they became the dominant flavor additive. Hops also had a preservative effect by limiting spoilage by bacteria. This not only made the beer more stable and attractive to the drinker, but also allowed the brewer to make a brew that was weaker than competing ales. Since prices were very rigidly controlled, this made beer more profitable than ale in the fifteenth and sixteenth centuries.

Other herb and spice flavorings largely disappeared in England through the seventeenth and eighteenth centuries, and thereafter they were used mainly only in certain beers in Belgium, such as the famous *wits*. However, in England one beer, Devon White, was flavored with *gruit* (as mixtures of herb flavorings were called) and did survive into the nineteenth century.[3] The use of various herb and spice flavorings has enjoyed a small revival in some of the specialty beers, particularly Christmas ales, produced by American microbreweries.

Despite the advent of hops, ale lived on for many centuries, most notably in country house breweries, virtually all of which maintained a brew house to cater to both the owners and the staff. At some stage, as the commercial or common brewers produced only beer, country house ale became a hopped brew, but it still kept the original name.

Eventually, the term *ale* came back into general fashion to refer to strong beers. By the eighteenth century, the ale brewed in private houses often came from the first runnings of the wort from a mash, meaning that it was the strongest brew.[4] Second runnings would yield beer, a weaker beverage, and subsequent runnings would yield the much weaker small beer, suitable for the lowest servants to drink. Note that at that time, the hydrometer had not been invented, so no method existed for measuring the strength of wort or beer. (The hydrometer had been suggested for this purpose in 1760 and was used by James Baverstock, a professional brewer, in 1769. Use of this instrument was put on a firm technological basis as a brewer's tool by John Richardson, a brewing author, in his 1786 *Statical Estimates*.[5])

Thus the terms *strong* and *weak* were purely relative. Extant recipes from the early nineteenth century suggest that ale first runnings were at around an original gravity of 1.111 (27.1 °P), second at about 1.075 (18.2 °P), and third at 1.040 (10.0 °P).[6] Few modern beers would match the gravities of these first two, while the third is pretty close to the average for all English beers today!

In the eighteenth century, ales, as very strong brews, were frequently drunk from small, liqueur-sized glasses, often of very fancy style and sometimes etched with barley and hop motifs. They were treated with the same care as imported wines and served only from fine glass decanters (if only some of today's wine snobs could be made to realize this!). The Bass Museum in Burton-upon-Trent displays a pair of glass decanters from the 1760s, one engraved "ALE" and the other "BEER."

But I still haven't addressed the origin of pale ale. As many writers have pointed out, *pale* merely meant that it was less dark than other beers. Prior to the eighteenth century, most of these "pale" ales would have been what today is called brown ale. One reason for this is that malting techniques made it difficult to avoid some roasting, or even scorching, of the malt, thereby making it quite dark. Pale malt could be made with coke as fuel, since a coke fire was easier to control than those made from the more commonly used wood or straw. However, coke was not readily available until the early eighteenth century. (It was used a little in the early seventeenth century but did not apparently find great favor. [7]) The first commercially successful coking facility was started in 1709 and by 1713, coke was being used in iron smelting.[8]

Coke-drying of malt seems to have been used more in the North and Midlands of England, rather than in the Southeast, where large-scale commercial brewing was taking place. Private house brewers apparently preferred coke-dried malt, and they might have been the major producers of pale ale in the late sixteenth and early seventeenth centuries.[9] Since these would have been wealthy people, this accords with the idea that pale ale was a drink for the rich, rather than for the poor. As is shown later in this chapter, this might have played a big part in the development of the style in the nineteenth century.

Pale ale reportedly was sold in London as early as 1623, at the Peacock Inn, Gray's Inn Lane. The record simply said "Burton Ale," which later evidence suggests was more likely a dark brown beer.[10] Pale ale brewers prospered in London around the end of the seventeenth century, with some of this coming from Nottingham and Burton.[11] However, it seems likely that the Burton brewers continued to brew mainly dark beers until the early nineteenth century; the Bass brewery, for example, produced its first pale ale in 1823.[12] However, Derbyshire brewers were coke-drying malt.[13] This meant that their beer could well have been pale in color. Probably the same applied to Nottingham beer, since this city sat in the middle of a coal-mining area.

Most London brewers produced brown beers. Around 1700, these beers encountered intense competition from pale ales, despite the fact that pale ales were more expensive to produce. Adding to the high price of pale ales were transportation costs if a pale ale was imported from outside the city, and especially if it came from the North. Yet, pale ale seems to have increased in popularity from 1710 to 1720 in the Capital.[14] As evidence of this, when Eliot's Stag Brewery in Pimlico was rebuilt in 1715, it had two brew houses, including one called the Pale Brewhouse.[15] (Stag, much later, became Watney's, which until recently was one of England's biggest brewers. In the 1990s, it gave up brewing for pub owning.)

It might have been this pressure from pale ale brewers that led to the development of porter as a way for brown beer producers to counteract what could have been a major threat to their business. However, that is another story. It is certainly true that after about 1720, porter became the most popular beer in London and later in the rest of the country. Later in the century, porter brewers such as Whitbread, Thrale, and Meux became the first really large-scale brewing companies, turning out hundreds of thousands of barrels annually. There were ale brewers other than Eliot in London, but in general their outputs were much smaller than those of the great porter brewers, none of them having reached even 30,000 barrels of output by 1800.[16] Note, too, that although brewing in Burton probably goes back to the eleventh century, when an abbey was founded there, by the eighteenth century Burton brewers were producing on a much smaller scale than the London porter brewers. For example, in 1786 Bass had total sales of fewer than 500 barrels, about what a reasonably sized modern American brewpub might turn out! At that stage, Bass was one of the smaller Burton brewers, but even the larger ones, such as Benjamin Wilson, were producing only around 2,000 barrels in 1790.[17]

The Arrival of India Pale Ale

In 1752, George Hodgson opened an ale brewery in Bow, in the East End of London. Then, in 1790, in what was a major event in the evolution of pale ale, he began shipping pale ale to India. Author Charles Stuart Calverley immortalized this innovation in blank verse:

Oh Beer! O Hodgson, Guinness, Allsopp, Bass!
Names that should be on every infant's tongue!

Beginning in 1799, Barclay, Perkins—the successor to Thrale's great porter brewery—brewed an India pale ale. So did several Scottish breweries, although these probably never obtained a significant share of the East India export trade.[18] Another source suggests that John Eliot was among the first brewers to ship beer to East India and that India ale was a significant business for him almost from the time when he took over the Stag Brewery in 1788.[19] That might suggest that he was brewing India ale before Hodgson and was not just a competitor of his. However, I have not found anything to support this contention, and I am sure that Watney's, the subsequent owners of the Stag Brewery, would have capitalized on the idea of their predecessor's having beaten Hodgson to the punch.

Hodgson was a very astute businessman when it came to handling actual and potential competitors. He used all sorts of tricks, such as flooding the East India market to drive down the price whenever competitors tried to move in and then raising the price again when they backed away. He even set up his own East India import business, run by his son.[20]

The East India market for beer was not new; as early as 1697, about 700 barrels per year were being exported there.[21] By 1750, this figure had almost doubled, although it might have been mainly porter, rather than pale ale, that was shipped. Fifty years later, the number of barrels soared (comparatively speaking) to 9,000. Probably mostly bottled beer was exported, this at a time when bottling was not a normal practice for brewers, since bottling made the beer relatively expensive. What made the East India trade attractive to brewers was low transportation costs. Low costs were possible because the return journey was profitable to shippers, when they brought back exotic spices, silks, jewels, and other valuable goods. Hodgson's ability to capitalize on this was a further example of his business acumen.

Hodgson was smart enough to realize that he could dominate the market by designing a beer specifically for this trade, rather than just shipping his standard beers, which were brewed for the home market. In this sense, he was clearly the first man to brew what we now call an India pale ale, although it is possible that other brewers shipped pale ale to India before Hodgson. Not a lot is known about this beer, for no recipes remain, but it appears that he did make it much hoppier and more bitter than was then customary for ales. He probably also

Reproducing an Eighteenth-Century Beer

Dr. John Harrison is perhaps the foremost expert on reviving old English beers by deciphering brewers' books. I recommend you read his article on this topic in the *Brewer's Guardian*.[22] There, he explains just how difficult this is, even when you have your hands on an eighteenth-century brewer's recipe! He and a group of English brewers have done a lot of very good work, not only in researching old recipes, but also in translating them into recipes suitable for homebrewing using modern ingredients. They have published a recipe for this beer in their book *Old British Beers and How to Make Them*.[23]

This recipe cites an original gravity of 1.070 (17.5 °P) and a hop rate of 2.5 ounces of Kent Goldings per gallon. At 5% alpha acid, a fairly common level for Goldings, this represents 62.5 hop bitterness units (HBU) per 5 gallons (converting to U.S. gallons). Even allowing for relatively poor utilization at such high hop rates, these values calculate to an improbable 200 international bitterness units (IBU) for this beer—by any standards, even 50 IBU would make a very bitter beer. So this beer should be undrinkable according to modern palates. However, I made a full-mash version of this beer, adjusting malt levels to correspond to the extraction rate I get and hop rates to give around 200 IBU (calculated) at a 20% utilization rate, rather than those indicated by Harrison, so as to achieve an original gravity of 1.070 (17.5 °P). Here's my version of the recipe for 5 U.S. gallons.

Original IPA

Two-row English pale
malt (2.5 °SRM)   10.2 lb. (4.6 kg)

English Kent Goldings hops
(7.8% alpha acid)
Bittering   4.7 oz. (134 g)
Aroma   1.0 oz. (28 g)

Pale malt mashed with gypsum-hard water at 153 °F (67.3 °C), boiled 90 minutes with bittering hops at start, aroma hops at knockout. Top-fermenting yeast (Ringwood in my case), two weeks in primary, 10 days in secondary, and then bottled with low-level priming sugar (0.5 ounces, 14 grams) or cane sugar.

This is indeed a bitter beer. But there is a good deal of malt body to balance the bitterness. And, in the true spirit of an IPA, it should be well matured—at least six months; the keeping tends to modify the bitterness. The end product is a beer that takes a little getting used to but that is rewarding in its complexity. Sipped slowly in company with a good strong cheese like a really sharp Vermont Cheddar, or better still an English Stilton, it provides a very rewarding experience.

In May 1994, the British Guild of Beer Writers staged a conference on IPA, at which Dr. Harrison provided samples of his re-creation of Hodgson's IPA. It was apparently six weeks old when presented. Reporters on the conference variously characterized the dry-hopped beer as having a powerful Goldings hop aroma and an intense bitterness![24] This might seem a short time for the maturation of a strong beer like this, but Harrison pointed out that the average time for the journey from India to England was 36 days. It could therefore have been on sale in India approximately six weeks after brewing. Another presenter at the conference, Richard Wilson, put a different view on this. He reportedly stated that true IPAs were "keeping" or "vatted" beers. In other words, they were matured for long periods before shipping.

I do not now whether Hodgson matured his beers at the brewery. He was a smart enough businessman to realize that he would make money more quickly if he shipped the beer as soon as it was brewed. He might have felt that the turbulence and temperature changes involved in a five- to six-week journey to India on a sailing ship was more than enough maturation period for his beer!

made it weaker than was customary for ales, although what was "weaker" is unclear. Dr. John Harrison has suggested that Hodgson's India Ale had an original gravity of 1.070 (17 °P). This compares with strong ale, which he suggests had an original gravity of 1.110 (27 °P), and to common ale, at 1.075 (18 °P)—the latter would be considered a strong brew today!

We can only guess at what hop varieties Hodgson would have used. Goldings, which was probably grown only in Kent, was introduced in the 1780s and subsequently became the prime pale ale hop. However, the ale brewers of London and the surrounding area used only hops from Farnham in Surrey, while Kentish hops were largely used by the porter brewers.[25] Whatever hop varieties were used, we do not know what their alpha acid levels were. Nor do we know whether they were used fresh and, if not, just how they were stored. Since there was no such thing as refrigeration at the time, stored hops would likely have been very low in alpha acid. Harrison indicates that Hodgson used new season hops for pale ales and old hops for porter brewing.[26] He also quotes Hodgson as using a hopping rate of 22 pounds per quarter (330 pounds) of malt. This equals approximately 10.5 ounces per 5 U.S. gallons, or close to 70 ounces per U.S. barrel, at a starting gravity of 1.070 (17.5 °P).

Burton Brewers and the Rise of Pale Ale

As indicated earlier in this chapter, at the end of the eighteenth century brewing in Burton was small-scale stuff compared to that of the great London porter brewers. At that time, the eight Burton breweries *combined* managed to produce only about 20,000 barrels a year. Meanwhile, the porter brewers were pushing into the frontiers of brewing technology, introducing the use of scientific instruments such as the thermometer and the hydrometer and adopting mechanical advances such as the steam engine, first installed by a London brewer in 1784. Porter was the dominant beer, popular everywhere in the country, as well as in London; it was even being brewed in Ireland. The population of London had grown rapidly in the eighteenth century, as the Industrial Revolution got under way, and many people left the land to work in the factories of the bigger cities. That meant the London brewers had a huge market literally on their doorstep. This was a great advantage in a time when transporting a high-volume product was difficult, slow, and expensive.

Although Burton brewers exported to London, the trade was small. By the time the product reached the city, it cost too much for it to be sold in quantity. For most of the second half of the eighteenth century, pressures on costs had been small, and the price of porter had remained remarkably stable. So the Burton brewers looked in a different direction. They could transport their beer cheaply by water, thanks to the introduction of the River Trent navigation system. This system linked them directly to the east coast port of Hull, through a canal/river route. This enabled them to build a trade with countries around the Baltic Sea, especially Russia.

As already discussed, this Russian trade was with a strong brown beer, perhaps sweeter than porter. It is unclear what *brown* really meant then, and in fact the term *nut brown* is used quite often in the literature. That suggests to me it was fairly light brown, rather than dark like a porter. Benjamin Wilson received complaints from Baltic merchants in 1793 that his ale was dark compared to that of his competitors.[27] So the standard color was probably at least a moderate brown, rather than dark brown or black. In my youth, I remember Ind Coope, Allsopp's offering "Burton" as a special winter ale. I do not remember much else about it, except that it was definitely a dark ale. In 1948, brown ale in England was defined as a filtered, carbonated, and bottled mild ale, "but it may also be a beer of the Burton type."[28] The same writer says that "Burton is a strong ale of pale ale type, but made with a proportion of highly dried or slightly roasted malts; it is consistently darker in colour and with a fuller flavour than the pale ales." The one remaining modern English beer from this Russian export trade is the seldom brewed Courage Russian Imperial Stout, a very dark beer that was brewed in London until recently, when its production was moved to Yorkshire.

Although Burton's trade with the Baltic countries and Russia was steady, it did not represent huge quantities of beer. Benjamin Wilson's brewery had the largest share, exporting around 2,000 barrels to the Baltic in 1790. Bass, later the world's largest brewer for a time, shipped only 211 barrels in the same year. One advantage to the Burton brewers of this trade was that they were able to bring back German, Russian, and Polish oak suitable for making beer casks. These types of oak are very dense, and when the casks were properly coopered, they would not have permitted significant leaching of tannins from the wood.

Around the turn of the eighteenth century, things began to change. Although not obvious at the time, porter had just about reached its peak in terms of popularity, for several reasons. Perhaps the main one was cost. The Napoleonic Wars caused a number of economic problems in England, one consequence of which was sky-rocketing barley and malt prices. Another reason was that as porter brewers became more technologically sophisticated, they realized that brown malt gave lower extract yields than did pale malt. Since brown malt was also sold in smaller unit quantities, it was more expensive in terms of cost of extract. The brewers sought less costly ways to create the typical flavor of porter. However, they were not really successful until malt-roasting techniques were developed around 1820. Meanwhile, many unscrupulous publicans and some brewers saved money by adulterating their porter with all sorts of nasty chemicals, drugs, and herbal extracts. As a result, porter started to develop a bad name among drinkers and to decline in popularity, thus opening the door to ale brewers.

Because of the Napoleonic Wars, the Baltic Sea was blockaded to English ships in 1806. Even when this blockade was lifted, various decrees by the European nations in 1807 severely curtailed English trade into the Baltic, including the trade of the Burton brewers with Russia. Further competition to the Burton brewers came from the establishment of a porter brewery in Russia. A Mr. Stein in St. Petersburg built this in the period 1810–1820.[29] The loss of the Baltic trade did not hit all Burton brewers badly. Benjamin Wilson, who had the greatest share of trade with Russia, was the brewer who suffered the most. Michael Bass, in contrast, suffered less.

He had tried to compete with Wilson in the Baltic, but failing that, had concentrated on the English markets.[30] Bass's failure to obtain a share of the Baltic market was a blessing in disguise; when IPA began to be produced in Burton, Bass had a sound base from which to expand. On the other hand, Benjamin Wilson was so discouraged by the difficulties of trading caused by the Napoleonic blockade, that in 1806 he passed the brewery on to his nephew, Samuel Allsopp.

After the Napoleonic Wars ended in 1815, high tariffs imposed by the Baltic countries prevented any great resumption of the ale trade. Also important at this time was that in 1813, the East India Company, which handled all shipping to India, lost its monopoly on the Indian trade.[31] This was significant because it was the East India Company that apparently persuaded the Burton brewers to produce India ale in the first place. Its lost monopoly was perhaps the first step in the loosening of George Hodgson's firm grip on the export trade to India. In 1821, a director of the East India Company, Mr. Marjoribanks (pronounced Marchbanks), complained to Samuel Allsopp about his dissatisfaction with Hodgson: ". . . [he] has given offense to most of the merchants of India."[32] But Marjoribanks pointed out that beer in the standard dark, sweet Burton style was not an acceptable substitute for

Hodgson's India Ale. He later sent Allsopp a dozen bottles of Hodgson's ale to show him what he was looking for.[33]

It is not apparent whether Marjoribanks had any personal ax to grind in this affair. Had he argued with Hodgson? Did he have any relationship with Allsopp? Was he looking for some kind of political edge within the company? Or had Hodgson simply exceeded his position and tried to go around the East India Company? Or did Marjoribanks just see this as a way of reviving the ailing fortunes of the company, now that it had lost its monopoly position? George's Porter Brewery of Bristol attempted to make India ale in 1828, and a senior partner in the brewery commented about Hodgson's version: "We neither like its thick and muddy appearance or rank bitter flavour."[34] So perhaps Marjoribanks was simply dissatisfied with the quality of the beer Hodgson was shipping to India.

Allsopp supposedly took the samples of India ale to his brewer Job Goodhead and asked him if he could produce a malt that would yield a similar pale beer. Goodhead said he could and is supposed to have made a trial small-scale brew using a teapot. This story might be apocryphal, or at least slightly embellished, since it did not emerge until recounted to a historian some 30 years later. Nevertheless, the first full-scale brew was made in 1822, and the first shipment to India of Allsopp's India pale ale was in 1823.[35]

Allsopp was not the only brewer trying to get in on Hodgson's act. Charles McMaster reported that the first IPA brewed in Edinburgh, Scotland, was made by the Edinburgh-Leith Brewery in 1820. It used much lower hopping rates than Hodgson did: 8 pounds per quarter of malt, compared to Hodgson's 22 pounds per quarter![36] Bass is also reported to have commenced brewing IPA in 1823.[37] In 1827, a cargo of its IPA destined for India was shipwrecked, salvaged, and auctioned off in Liverpool. Local drinkers reportedly were so delighted with the beer that they demanded it should become readily available on the home market.

The drive towards Burton production of pale ales might have come much earlier. In 1793, Wilson (whom Allsopp succeeded) received complaints from his Baltic customers that his ale was much darker than that of his rivals. In order to sell in England, it needed to be paler to compete with the increasingly popular ales of London and the South-Eastern counties. As a result, Allsopp wrote to his various English customers in 1808, asking "whether pale ale or that of a darker colour is most liked with you." Further, the Liverpool market required a more bitter beer than was the case with Burton ales at this stage. London was also requiring more bitter beers from Burton.[38]

But Michael Bass was in an expansion mode also, establishing export beachheads in parts of the world not yet reached by other English brewers. For example, in 1806 his brewery exported about 8% of its output to London. By 1820, this figure had risen to 20%. However, trade with Liverpool was almost as important. Much of what was sent there was then exported to America (the first shipment of five casks went to America in 1795), the West Indies, and Australia.[39] Unlike his father, who founded the brewery and also ran a carrier business, Michael Bass was an ambitious man who had only the brewery to support his aspirations. He very soon became the major exporter of East India pale ale, as it was called for a time.

From 1832 to 1833, approximately 12,000 barrels of English beer were exported to India. Of that total, Bass shipped 5,200 barrels and Allsopp 1,400, while Hodgson managed a still very respectable 3,600.[40] According to an exhibit in the Bass Museum, by 1842 Hodgson was no longer exporting to India, having been pushed out of the market by the superior ales of Burton brewers.

But the India business was still a relatively small amount of Bass's total trade. By 1839, Bass's annual output

A Direct Link to the Past

Worthington White Shield was brewed continuously since probably the 1820s and survived Worthington's merger with Bass in the early twentieth century. It was fermented in Burton Unions, but more important, it was a bottle-conditioned beer. Bottle-conditioned beers were very unusual, so much so that in the 1930s Bass actually issued written instructions for pouring White Shield. Bass further designed a special glass that held exactly one bottleful—it was called, not surprisingly, the Worthington. By the 1970s, bottle-conditioned beer was very rare in England, although it has enjoyed something of a revival in the 1990s.

When shipped to bottlers, the beer included detailed instructions calling for the casks to sit for 7 to 14 days, depending on the season, before bottling. This waiting period was to be followed by 4 to 5 weeks in the bottle before sale.[41] Because the journey to India took 5 to 6 weeks, the beer would be drunk at least 10 weeks after leaving England. Thus, it was fairly well-matured even if it was not kept at the brewery for any length of time (which it probably was anyway).

Although the pedigree of this White Shield might go back to the early Burton IPAs, the recipe for it surely changed over time. It ceased to be brewed in Burton when Bass closed down its union fermenting system in the 1980s, being produced first in

English IPAs from Burton-on-Trent.

Sheffield, and then in Birmingham (two other great city names of the English Industrial Revolution). The latest version of White Shield has an original gravity of 1.056 (14 °P), 40 IBU (using Northern Brewer and the American Eroica hops), and 10 °SRM color. Sadly, this also is the last version of this classic beer, for the final brew of the beer was sold in the fall of 1998.[42] Bass decided to part company with its origins, apparently because sales of White Shield were too low. However, Bass never put a fraction of the promotional muscle behind this historic beer that it did for its alcoholic lemonade, Hooch, or its nitrogen-dispensed pseudo-Irish pasteurized Caffreys "bitter."

was almost 31,000 barrels, about 17,000 of which was pale ale, with the rest being porter and Burton strong ale.[43] Clearly, Bass was selling the major part of his output in England. He was not unusual among English brewers, for even at the peak of the export trade in 1859, only about 2% of the total volume of beer brewed in England was exported.[44]

Other Burton brewers were turning out pale ales, most notably Salt and William Worthington, but their share of the East India market seems to have been small. Nevertheless, Worthington's IPA, called Worthington White Shield, captured a special niche in British brewing history.

Why Pale Ale Was a Success

There were many more factors that contributed to the success of pale ale than simply the brewers' recognition of the East India market as a substitute for their lost Baltic trade. These included the following:

- the quality of Burton water
- advances in brewing technology
- social changes in England
- critical mass of Burton brewers, poised for expansion

- expansion in total beer consumption
- demise of both private and publican brewers
- establishment of railways
- the move to the widespread use of glass in the construction of drinking vessels
- changes in taste that favored pale beers

The high sulfate/carbonate well water of Burton was ideal for the production of highly hopped pale beers with a clean, sharp bitterness. But this might have been less important than the fact that in the early nineteenth century, the Burton brewers were ready to expand. They had absorbed the lessons of a more scientific approach to brewing pioneered by the porter manufacturers. They developed their technology to a point where they could make a complete change from their standard product and take the next step up to becoming major players in the brewing game. In short, they were at the point of explosion, just as the porter brewers had been almost exactly a century earlier.

As the Industrial Revolution accelerated in the late eighteenth century, a new social phenomenon emerged—people with what we now call disposable income. While this was true for the working classes to a certain extent (especially after 1850), it was even more so for the rapidly growing middle class, which was becoming well-off enough to be choosy about what they drank, almost without regard for price. A result of this was an increase in beer consumption from the 1830s to the 1870s.[45] From 1810 to 1830 consumption was in the range of 34 to 36 U.S. gallons per capita and reached a peak of almost 49 U.S. gallons per capita by 1879.[46]

The English drinker was looking to buy his beer from a commercial brewer, and many more of them were living in cities than had previously been the case. They were moving away from the idea of brewing their own beer, just as publicans were realizing it was easier to sell other people's beer, rather than to brew their own. For example, around 1830 private brewing accounted for over 20% of beer produced in England, while publican brewers (or brewpubs in modern terminology) produced around 45% of the total beer sold in England.[47] This means that commercial, or common, brewers had only about one-third of the market. (However, this would not have been the case in London, where the great porter brewers had long dominated the market.)

By the 1860s, private brewing had declined steeply to less than 3% of the country's total beer output. This was because the owners of the great country houses no longer brewed as much beer as they turned to imported wines and as tea-drinking became fashionable. In addition, their social habits changed—they spent a good part of their time in their London houses, which did not have brewing facilities. Even the poorer classes were no longer brewing as much of their own beer. As they moved into the industrial areas, they no longer had access to the space and ingredients to brew their own. In addition, they were probably working such long hours that they needed to rely on commercial brewers for their beer needs.

Similarly, during the same time period publican brewers virtually disappeared from the scene. Their share of total beer output declined from 45% in 1830 to about 15% by 1880 and only around 5% by 1900.[48] The steepest drop-off occurred during the 1870s and 1880s, as the commercial brewers went on a buying spree for pubs. Not only did the commercial brewers take over the market, they also increased in both numbers and in rates of production.[49] This reflected a significant change in society, one that still continues as we rely on large companies for our supplies of everything from food to consumer goods, rather than producing them ourselves. The growth of modern microbreweries reflects a reaction to this trend, that of our acceptance of industrial rather than craft products.

Also significant to the success of pale ale was the arrival of the railroad in England. It changed the face of transportation, particularly where bulky goods like beer were concerned. The main change for Burton brewers came in 1839, when the Derby to Birmingham line was opened. This line passed through Burton, giving the city a direct rail link to London and other cities, thereby allowing its beers, and those of Bass in particular, to establish a national reputation.[50] It was only a small step from there to the modern concept of a nationally recognized brand.

The next element of the equation was the increase in the availability and use of glass for drinking vessels. Prior to 1840, glass vessels were heavily taxed and so were not in common use. Pewter and earthenware vessels were used in most pubs, and some publicans even used stone vessels marked with their names.[51] Once this tax was removed, glass vessels rapidly became popular. This quickly led to a greater appreciation of the clear, sparkling character of pale ales, especially of those from Burton.

In addition, for reasons that are not clear, public taste had changed, and pale beers became more popular, as opposed to the darker porters and stouts. As stated previously, some of this was a social change. However, there was also a world move to pale beers, as exemplified by the emergence of pale lager in Pilsen, Czech Republic. Pale lagers rapidly pushed out brown beers in Europe, and not very much later became popular in America.

What's in a Barrel?

The capacity of a barrel has varied over the centuries. In the seventeenth century, a standard ale barrel held 32 gallons, while the beer barrel held 36 gallons. In 1688, both were changed to hold 34 gallons. In 1803, the capacities for both were increased to 36 gallons. Finally, in 1824 the barrel was set at the capacity that it still holds today: 36 imperial gallons. However, the barrel based on the imperial gallon was actually 16% less in volume than the 36-gallon barrel previously used.[52] Clearly, this variability complicates the deciphering of old recipes!

Whatever the reasons, Burton brewers prospered in the latter part of the nineteenth century. They moved away from the production of brown beers; by 1845, for example, pale ale at Bass accounted for about 73% of total production.[53] In 1853, Bass built a second brewery, and yet another in 1863. By 1876, it had become the world's largest brewer, quoted by one source as brewing about a million barrels annually (with Allsopp's a good second in the race, at 900,000 barrels).[54] Another source, however, cites just fewer than 900,000 barrels for Bass in 1876,

The Wadworth Brewery in Devizes, Wiltshire, has one of the most attractive brewery exteriors you will ever see.

with the 1 million–barrel mark reached in 1890.[55]

A significant development in the pale ale story was that brewers in the rest of the country soon jumped on the bandwagon. They began brewing their own versions of the style, turning out pale beers of a more wide-ranging character, some perhaps more or less hoppy, others perhaps darker than the Burton classic. The importance of this was that it meant that as the broader pale ale category emerged, IPA, as such, was no longer the dominant style. It became a substyle rather than the model. East India exports became a lesser part of the Burton brewers' total exports. By 1844, Bass shipments to Australia were almost at the same level as those to East India. (But perhaps this is not so surprising, since Bass began shipping to New South Wales in 1798.)[56] Foster's of Australia produced an IPA in the 1890s, emphasizing the establishment of the style in that country.[57] In the Fremantle History Museum in Western Australia, I also came across a 1903 photograph showing a Fremantle pub with an advertisement for Port Brewery Pale Ale.

What were the great porter brewers doing in the face of this stiff competition from Burton? Quite simply, they had to change in order to survive. Although still producing porter in quantity, many moved into ale brewing, at first brewing mainly a dark mild ale (probably a lighter-hopped, less-matured version of porter at this stage). But soon they were making pale ales also; Whitbread, for example, was brewing pale ale in the 1860s. Interestingly, they treated their brewing "liquor" by adding gypsum, an indication of how far technical knowledge of the brewing process had progressed by this stage.[58]

Other porter brewers reacted somewhat differently. They opened their own breweries in Burton, thereby taking advantage both of Burton's water quality and its well-established reputation for high-quality beer. These included Ind Coope in 1856 (which later merged with Allsopp in 1934); Mann, Crossman, and Paulin in 1872 and Truman in 1873 (both were later swallowed up by Watney's); and Charrington in 1872. Even Boddington's from Manchester got into the act, opening its Burton brewery in 1875. (This company still exists but only as a pub owner. Whitbread now operates Boddington's Manchester brewery and supplies it with beer!)

I have already pointed out that the Edinburgh brewers joined the trend much earlier with their own versions of IPA. Indeed, the Scottish brewers were technologically well advanced. They were the first to adopt several new techniques such as sparging and bottling on a fairly large scale in the 1860s—thirty years before it became common practice in England.[59] But IPA was also brewed in the Yorkshire city of Bradford. And after 1875, Newcastle brewers were also turning out their own versions of East India pale ale. This beer corresponded to the Edinburgh versions rather than to those of Burton. However, a bottler in the city offered not only "Pale India Ale," but also a "High-hopped India Pale Ale," although it is not clear whether the latter was actually brewed in Newcastle.[60] Other cities noted for pale ale brewing were Tadcaster in Yorkshire and Alton in Hampshire.

Burton remained a major brewing center and continued to improve its brewing technology by embracing the burgeoning science of chemistry and employing some of the best brewing scientists of the time—notably Horace Brown at Worthington. Bass still exported significant quantities of beer, especially to America and Canada. It had agents and bottlers in New York, Boston, and

Newark, as well as Winnipeg and Edmonton in Canada, and dealt with a bottler in Denver. In 1890, Bass registered the first three trademarks ever issued, the first for its pale ale and the next two for Burton Ale. The company went to great lengths to protect its labels. For example, in 1895 it sued the Avon Company of Baltimore for forging the famous Bass Red Triangle label. For similar forgery offenses, it acted against John H. Sutcliff of Albany, New York, and against Abraham Q. Wendell of Boston, who actually got five months hard labor for the crime![61]

But by the 1880s–1890s, Burton had lost its supremacy in the pale ale industry. Its brewers were clearly feeling the pinch of intense competition, both at home and abroad. In 1886, Bass and Allsopp had agreed to fix their prices on pale ales and further agreed that they would not try to undercut price by offering pale ales having a starting gravity below 1.050 (12.5 °P).[62] Taxation also became a factor in Burton's decline as countries adopted tariffs to protect their own breweries. From July 1899 to July 1900, Bass exported 100,000 gallons to India, while Younger's of Alloa in Scotland exported 260,000 gallons and the Kaiser Brewery of Pilsen 205,000 gallons.[63]

The Kaiser shipments are significant. The brewing of lager had become widely adopted, perhaps most notably in America, as far as Burton exports were concerned. When

Bass and Allsopp started their great expansions in the 1820s, Pilsener beers did not exist. The German and Austrian brewing industries, although long-established, were fragmented. Individual breweries were much smaller than the great companies of England that had led the way during the Industrial Revolution. Further, they were generally making brown beers because they did not know how to produce pale malts. Anton Dreher of Vienna and Gabriel Sedlmayer of Munich visited England on two occasions in the 1830s. Their mission was to learn English brewing technology, and they reportedly carried a hollowed-out walking stick to store surreptitiously obtained samples! Dreher later tried to brew an English ale in Vienna, but apparently it did not sell well. He then made a bottom-fermented lager using a pale malt, which married the clean lager flavor with the coppery color of a pale ale.[64] In 1842, the first Pilsener was brewed in the Bohemian town of Pilsen, and the style soon became favored in Germany.

Not long after that, a great migration of German peoples to America occurred. Several of the immigrants were brewers, and they took with them their methods for brewing the new lager beer. Soon ale brewers in America had a strong new competitor, as did the Burton brewers exporting to this country. I look at that in more detail later in this chapter.

What Exactly Was a Burton IPA

No known records remain of any of the original Burton IPAs. But by examining subsequent published information, one can guess what they might have been. Initially, IPA was not brewed in Burton Unions. (The Burton Union System is a fermentation system in which fermenting beer overflows a wooden cask via a swan neck and is recycled back into the cask.) Instead, the "dropping" system of fermentation was used. In this system, the beer is allowed to ferment in an open vat (called a round or square) and then is dropped into a cask for cleansing— that is, a finishing fermentation during which the bulk of the yeast settles out. Such a system would have created problems with beer clarity and loss of beer if the original yeast was powdery and nonflocculent, as was certainly the case later on.

The Burton Union System was invented by a Scotsman, Peter Walker, in Liverpool in 1838.[65] He apparently patented his "union set" system before moving to Burton and opening his own brewery there in 1846 and setting up his own system. This system was probably fairly crude at first, but it did allow for better recycling of the beer that overflows from the bung hole of the cask. The system's name comes from the fact that sets of casks are joined in "union" by a system of pipes and buckets.[66] Presumably, the other Burton brewers soon picked up on the method and later refined it by introducing the famous swan necks, by which the overflow of yeasty beer was fed into an overhead barm trough, where the yeast could be separated and the cleaned beer returned to the cask.

However, there are some discrepancies in the timing of the introduction of the union system to Burton. One source says Bass began using unions around 1840.[67] Another very respected beer historian indicates that the London brewer Whitbread used a type of union system as

The Burton Union sets in the yard of the Bass Museum at Burton-on-Trent. Only Marston's still operates unions, which were once the only way to brew an IPA in Burton!

early as the eighteenth century.[68] And a picture from Corran's *A History of Brewing* (from *Rees's Cyclopedia*, 1819–1820) shows a type of union system, with beer fermenting in round vats and overflowing into a collection vessel, a somewhat cruder system than that later used in Burton. Perhaps unions were something that just evolved as brewers tried to develop ways to avoid beer loss in their search for greater efficiencies and profits. It is difficult to see how other brewers could have used unions if Walker held a patent on them, but perhaps this is just another example of the difficulty of accurately pinning down the history of brewing.

Certainly brewers were looking at other ways of efficiently handling fermentation. Some involved various mechanical methods of skimming the excess yeast from the surface of the beer (remember, I am talking about top-fermented beers, where the yeast migrates to the surface at the end of fermentation). Brewers in the Yorkshire town of Tadcaster adopted a more individual approach. Called the Yorkshire stone square system, it initially employed vessels made from slate. Like the union system, it was a circulation system, differing primarily in that it involved the rousing of the yeast. This rousing was required because the strain that these brewers used was highly flocculent and tended to settle out before fermentation was complete.

It is well established that the union system became the preferred approach for brewing Burton pale ales. It permitted the efficient use of the powdery Burton yeast, and because this yeast was very slow to settle out of the beer, it allowed for very good fermentation attenuation. This high level of attenuation became a clear trait of Burton pale ales, resulting not only in a dry-tasting beer, but also emphasizing its hoppy character and bitterness.

In 1881, finishing gravities of Burton pale ales were around one-quarter to one-fifth of the starting gravity.[69] Careful chemical analyses of Burton pale ale indicate that attenuation might have been higher than this, going down from a starting gravity of 1.062 (15 °P) to below 1.010 (2.5 °P). Modern authors have indicated that pale ales might have attenuated from original gravities of around 1.065 to 1.070 (16 to 17 °P) to as low as 1.007 (1.8 °P).[70] Another account, from Wahl-Henius (data from 1887–1908) quotes results of from 1.011 to 1.007 (2.8 to 1.8 °P) for Bass pale ales of the 1880s and 1890s, while a similar beer from 1901 finished as low as 1.0035 (0.9 °P).[71] These were presumably all bottled beers; a Bass draught pale ale had a higher finishing gravity at 1.014 (3.5 °P). Also interesting is that the Wahl-Henius list included pale ales from Hanover, Germany, and from the Norwegian Brewery Ringnes. Note that the Bass sample finishing at the lowest gravity came from a time when the brewer was almost certainly using sugar, which could well account for such a low finishing gravity.

It has been suggested that brewing sugar was used in the original IPAs.[72] Hodgson himself might have used sugar both in the malt bill and with the finings, although this seems highly unlikely.[73] Brewing sugar as a specialty product was not available at that time, and sugar as such was banned from use in brewing by the Customs and Excise in order to preserve the duties on malt. This ban on sugar was temporarily relaxed for a few years in the early nineteenth century, but it was soon restored. Not until 1847 was sugar finally permitted, up to a maximum of 25% of the grist, and it was taxed in a manner similar to malt.[74]

Because of the tax on sugar, its use was probably not favored at first. Eventually, its use did become more popular so that by 1878, it was being used in significant quantities, with total usage by English brewers amounting to 10% of malt consumption.[75] However, Bass was probably still using only malt since it had very extensive maltings of its own. At that stage, other adjuncts were not in use, but more on that later.

IPAs in the first half of the nineteenth century were produced from pale malt only. Burton maltsters were experts at their trade, and it has been suggested that they made a special "white malt" for East India pale ale and their superior pale ales.[76] Original gravities were from 1.060 to 1.072 (14.7 to 17.5 °P), with an average of 1.068 (16.5 °P) for export ales in 1846.[77] However, one recipe for pale ale during that time had an original gravity of 1.075 (18.2 °P).[78] Also worth noting is that these gravities remained virtually constant until around the end of the century. However, in 1865–1866 Bass produced no fewer than 19 different ales, as well as several types of porter![79] Original gravities of the nonexport beers are not recorded and might have been well outside of the range quoted here.

A lot of information is available on hopping rates. John Tuck, in *Private Brewer's Guide to the Art of Brewing Ale and Porter,* quotes 2.3 pounds/barrel of "bright East Kents," which runs out at 4.3 ounces per 5 U.S. gallons.[80] The alpha acid content of these hops is unknown, but even assuming only 4% and a utilization of 25%, the result would be about 65 IBU in the finished beer—a fairly high value by modern standards. In 1881, higher hopping rates were reported—around 3.3 pounds/barrel, or 6.2 ounces per 5 U.S. gallons, which would be close to 95 IBU using the same assumptions.[81] In 1871, Bass used 20 pounds of hops per quarter of malt in export pale ale at an original gravity of 1.065 (15.8 °P) and a lower rate of 16 pounds/quarter for domestic pale ale at the higher gravity of 1.070 (17 °P).[82] For the export ale, this represents a hop rate of about 5 pounds/barrel, or just over 9 ounces per 5 U.S. gallons, which would give about 125 IBU at 4% alpha acid and 25% utilization.

Clearly, these beers were very bitter compared to modern styles. Of course, utilization rates were probably lower than 25%, but alpha acid values could have been higher than 4%. Although the chemistry of hops was not known at that time, there was some intuitive understanding of it. An 1880s writer, visiting the Bass breweries, described the hop store as being cool and dry, with daylight religiously excluded, although of course there was no refrigeration.[83] It is generally assumed that only English hops, and more specifically Kent Goldings, were used for IPAs. But that was certainly not the case with Bass. In 1860–1862, it used a combination of Hungarian barley and American hops, with the latter giving an unpleasant flavor reminiscent of black currants.[84] Even in the twentieth century, English brewers rather condescendingly refer to "the American flavor" conferred by hops from America. But this did not stop Bass from using American hops; in 1869, almost 50% of its hops consisted of imports from Germany and California.[85] This trend seems to have continued throughout the remainder of the nineteenth century and might be an important link between classic pale ales and some of the new versions of American IPAs, as discussed later in this chapter.[86]

But let's return to the original Burton IPAs. They were dry hopped, meaning hops were added to the cask during maturation to provide a strong hop aroma. For example, in 1881 the amount used by Burton brewers was as much as 2 pounds/barrel, or just under 4 ounces per 5 U.S. gallons,[87] while Bass supposedly used half of this amount.[88] Both of these rates are very high by modern standards. The beers would have had a good deal of hop character, although one quite different from the flavors resulting from late hopping, a practice that was uncommon until the twentieth century. Dry hopping is still utilized by English brewers of traditional ale, although at much lower levels than those given here.

Burton IPAs also are reputed to have what is sometimes called the "Burton snatch." This is a sulfury flavor sometimes attributed to the effect of yeast on the sulfates in Burton water. In fact, it is unlikely that yeast could reduce sulfate to sulfide.[89] It is almost certainly a yeast-derived flavor note and is sometimes claimed to be found in such beers as Marston's Pedigree, which is brewed with yeast propagated in Burton Unions. I have never detected this flavor in a Burton-brewed beer, but that might mean only that I have a high threshold for sulfury flavors.

Other aspects of Burton IPA flavor might have come from long storage in wooden casks. The first question is whether there were any flavors derived from the oak used to make the casks. This seems highly unlikely. English oak was often used for casks, and it is very dense and impervious to liquids, thus making it perfect for beer storage. Although much of the oak used by Burton brewers came from Poland and Germany because of their early Baltic export trade, this oak was similar to English oak.

Another aspect is the possibility of flavor being affected by contamination. The original Burton IPAs were probably vatted beers; that is, they were matured at the brewery before being exported. Oddly, there is little in the literature regarding the length of such maturation periods. I have come across only one pertinent reference, but even it was at the quite late date of around 1900. It refers to a Bass "Export Pale Ale" as being two to three years old![90] I mentioned earlier in the chapter that the ale would have been at least six weeks in cask on the journey to India before bottling, and of course it likely would have been held at quite a high temperature. For most beers, storage in wood under these conditions means that wild yeast and bacterial infections might affect the beer flavor. Principal among these is *Brettanomyces*, the yeast responsible for the "horse blanket" flavor of Belgian lambic beers, and lactic acid from various lactobacilli. However, the very high hopping rate used by Burton brewers could have prevented the development of such flavors, and there is no evidence from the literature that these beers did suffer from these defects.

The issue of the color of Burton IPAs is interesting. IPA was often considered pale in comparison to the popular brown and black beers of the seventeenth and eighteenth centuries. Harrison's suggestion that the Burton brewers used white or very pale malt would indicate that IPA was quite pale. But even today, English pale malts are still high-dried, compared to lager malts, so they are relatively high in color (3–5 °SRM). At the original gravities quoted previously, Burton pale ales were likely at least a deep copper-red to amber color. Maillard reactions, which cause browning, are catalyzed by copper ions, and the Burton brewers—like other brewers in England in the nineteenth century—all used copper kettles. These copper kettles would have caused some darkening of the wort.[91]

The following is a summary of the Burton IPA style:

- brewed from only pale two-row malt
- original gravity 1.060–1.070 (14.8–17 °P)
- water very high in mineral content, especially calcium

(up to 350 parts per million, or ppm), sulfate (about 600 ppm), and carbonate (as much as 200 ppm)
- kettle hopped with 2–5 pounds/barrel, or 4–9 ounces per 5 U.S. gallons, probably similar to Goldings, and low in alpha acid (4–5%)
- perhaps 60–130 IBU
- dry-hopped in casks with 1–2 pounds/barrel, 2–4 ounces per 5 U.S. gallons, probably the same hops as in the kettle
- fermented with a nonflocculent yeast
- highly attenuated, finishing gravity in the range 1.007–1.012 (1.8–3.0 °P)
- might have been matured in wood for several months
- subjected to up to two months of rough traveling, some of it at high temperature
- copper to amber in color (possibly 8–20 °SRM)
- sulfury note in flavor
- perhaps also some low-level lactic acid flavor and a few *Brettanomyces* "horse blanket" flavor notes

In chapter 5, I give a recipe that might come close to these specifications. Or, for the more adventurous, you could use these to develop your own.

The Bitter End

Looking at modern English pale beers, such an emphasis on IPAs is not really warranted. The predominant beers of this type are now called bitter, and in general bear little resemblance to IPA as outlined in the previous summary. They are still highly hopped and bitter, but only by modern taste standards. While there are beers called IPA produced by brewers today, a survey showed that out of the thousand or so pale beers brewed in England in 1997, only 41 were designated IPA. The average gravity of these was only 1.041 (10.2 °P), and one was as low as 1.033 (8.3 °P). Bittering levels were only moderate. In short, if you will forgive the pun, they are a very pale reflection of the original. Bitter, once a minor subcategory of pale ale, is now often higher quality than its precursor's modern incarnations.

Why and how did this evolution occur? The reasons are many, with changes in taste being one of the most important. But perhaps the main ones are those of commercial and governmental pressures. By the end of the nineteenth century, beer in England had become an industrial product and was no longer representative of the output of a dedicated craftsman. This change had started with the porter brewers, who were the first to become large-scale producers and then had to adapt to meet the challenge of the loss of a stable selling price coupled with the loss of a stable ingredient cost.

One answer to this challenge was to decrease the amount of time spent maturing beers so as to ensure a faster turn-around and therefore a better cash-flow situation. In other words, they moved away from vatting their products and turned to making them running beers—that is, beers shipped from the brewery with minimal keeping time after fermentation. This was not easy to do technically in the eighteenth century, as a running beer lacked stability in the trade. Remember that at that time, fermentation was not well understood. Porters were fairly high-gravity beers and if shipped too soon could easily undergo refermentation in cask, thereby making them difficult to handle, muddy in appearance when served, and so on.

During the nineteenth century, brewers became not only larger, but also more technically aware, thus enabling them to skillfully control the processes of fermentation and maturation. There appears to have been a gradual trend towards the making of running beers, starting with the emergence of mild ales, which at the outset might simply have been running porters. One approach to this was to mix a running beer with a vatted one in order to confer the flavor of a long-matured beer onto one that had sat at the brewery for perhaps only a few weeks. This approach might have led to the development of the so-called "stock ales" in the last half of the eighteenth century. Greene, King in the county of Suffolk is one of England's major regional brewers. It still produces a strong pale ale vatted for a lengthy period and used for blending into other beers.[92]

The Burton brewers were not immune to this trend. In 1884, M. A. Bass, son of Michael Bass, commented "how fast our trade is becoming a running one." He said that all of Bass's pale ale had become running beer, except for that brewed in January to March.[93] This partly reflected the fact that export trade had become only a relatively small part of the company's business. This was especially true of the East India trade, which had become insignificant by then. Indeed, an 1879 Bass price list did not include an IPA at all, only a pale ale and an export ale![94] It is interesting that the Bass Ale sold in America today in bottles does have IPA on its label, although in very small type.

Competition among English brewers intensified. As a result, in the late nineteenth century many larger breweries became public companies, beginning with Guinness in 1886. Much of the money raised in this manner was used to buy public houses in order to "tie up" outlets for their beer. (The trend toward buying public houses had started earlier in some areas, particularly in London where property prices were high.) A brewer would lend publicans money to buy a public house on the condition that the house sell its beer exclusively. Often, if the publican could not make a go of the business, the brewer would become the owner of the property. From there, it was but a small step to a deliberate policy of buying public houses and building a whole tied estate.

The Lamb, a Young's pub in London, is near the main university buildings. In addition to the excellent beer, it is one of the very few remaining pubs that still have Victorian "snob screens" around the bar.

Brewers were spending a lot of money, and some public houses were going for remarkably high sums. A consequence of this was a decline in profitability for brewers, and even some bankruptcies. Allsopp of Burton was a prime example of this. Their chase after pubs left them unable to pay a dividend in 1901. By 1913, they were in receivership (this is somewhat equivalent to today's Chapter 11 bankruptcy).[95]

Further, during the second half of the nineteenth century brewers all over the country became adept at brewing the lighter pale ales. Even the so-called "country brewers" were more knowledgeable of the science of brewing. Many of them had grown to fair-sized concerns through take-overs of competitors in their local markets. This ensured regional brewers had a good home base from which to compete with other regional brewers and to establish footholds in the larger cities like London.

During this time, there were many scientific advances—most notably the use of refrigeration and the work of Louis Pasteur that showed the true role of yeast in fermentation, followed by Emil Hansen's isolation of single culture yeasts. Other developments included pasteurization and the mechanization of bottling. There were even advancements in filtration and artificial carbonation, although for a time much of the output of England's brewers was still draught beer in cask. Further, the role of water quality in brewing had become much clearer and the subsequent treatment of mash water with gypsum for the production of pale beers had become widespread.[96] The day of the brewer as chemist had dawned.

Competition, growth in brewery size, and scientific advances all led to a move away from the classic IPA style for many brewers. In what numerous people viewed as a lowering of quality (although the brewers themselves did not share that view), they sought ways to produce their beers more cheaply through the use of imported raw materials. As I pointed out earlier in the chapter, Bass (and presumably other brewers in Burton and elsewhere) used a good deal of imported hops, including those from America. But for many years, Bass had also imported considerable amounts of malting barley from countries such as France, Turkey, and Algeria, as well as California in America.[97] Brewers also investigated the use of other ingredients that would enable them to economize by reducing malt usage. These included sugar and other cereals. For example, in 1874 a Bass chemist patented a process for treating starch-containing substances that could be used as substitutes for malt.[98]

England never had anything like the German purity law, *Reinheitsgebot*. However, something similar had effectively been in place through taxation on malt and later hops. Malt was first taxed by Charles II in 1660. This tax was placed on a firmer footing in the eighteenth century, when legislation was introduced to prohibit the use of ingredients other than malt and hops. This ban was rigidly enforced by the Inland Revenue, which was responsible for collecting the tax and which in the early nineteenth century prosecuted many porter brewers accused of using toxic adulterants. In 1847, a change in the law permitted the use of sugar in brewing. This was the first real hole in the fabric of what had virtually amounted to an English purity law. Barley growers lobbied strongly against this change, especially after 1870 when their markets were being eroded by cheap imports.[99] They were themselves opposed by brewers who formed the Free Mash Tun Association to promote the use of adjuncts.[100]

Then, in 1880, an event happened that not only opened the gates to the use of malt substitutes, but ultimately led to the disappearance of IPA in its original style in Britain. The Free Mash Tun Act, introduced by then Prime Minister Sir William Gladstone, removed taxes on ingredients such as malt and hops, replacing them by a single tax based only on wort original gravity. Over the centuries, various British laws had affected brewers and drinkers—others continue to do so even today—but the 1880 act was, in my opinion, the most far-reaching. Its more important provisions included the following:

1. Homebrewers were taxed at the same rate as their commercial counterparts.
2. The Inland Revenue was newly concerned only with the wort, so brewers could obtain their extract from any source they wished.

3. The standard tax rate was based on an original gravity of 1.057 (14 °P); stronger beers were taxed at a higher rate, and weaker ones at a lower rate.

The first provision was perhaps the least important, since homebrewing had already greatly diminished, but this law was almost the last nail in its coffin. Homebrewing began to revive only in the 1950s, which was when I began brewing. Since the taxation provisions of the Free Mash Tun Act were repealed in 1963, it has flowered. As happened later in America, a renaissance in homebrewing in England preceded the renaissance in commercial craftbrewing.

The second provision was significant in clearing the way to the use of adjuncts. From 1900 to 1910, the use of sugar by English brewers escalated to around 30% of the total amount of malt, while the use of cereals increased to as much as 10% of the total.[101] By 1914, grist composition had settled out to the combination of 80% malt, with sugar and other cereals totaling about 20% of the grist, which is pretty much the case today. Big, modern, commercial brewers assert that using these adjuncts is essential because they are nitrogen diluents—that is, they lower the total protein content of the beer and prevent chill haze. But English traditional beers, and especially cask-conditioned real ales, should not be served cold. Rather they should be served at around 52–55 °F (11–13 °C). So this argument seems specious. Further, sugar and cereals are not adjuncts. The term *adjunct* implies that something was added. Sugar and cereals add nothing; they are merely cheap malt substitutes.

Perhaps the worst part of the Free Mash Tun Act was the third provision. The method of taxation, basing the tax rate on an established original gravity, put great pressure on brewers to ship their beer quickly and to reduce wort gravity below the standard 1.057 (14 °P). The effect of this provision was not instantaneous, partly because the figure selected was a real average for the time and partly because the actual level of taxation was no higher than that paid at the time on malt and hops. But taxation rates always tend to increase with time, and the English government preferred taxing beer because (a) it raised a lot of money quickly and (b) it allowed the government to take the moral high ground by saying it was controlling alcohol consumption.

By 1900, the average original gravity of English beers was still around 1.055 (13.6 °P). The Great War of 1914–1918 changed that. During the war, taxes rose steeply. By 1918, Bass, for example, was paying duty at the rate of about 20% of its total production costs. It's probably not surprising, then, that Bass ceased to brew high-gravity beers. Yet worse was to come. Immediately after the war, beer taxation began to increase rapidly. By 1921, the duty was 53% of Bass's total production costs![102]

This trend was to continue. So did the move towards lower original gravities, accelerated in part by shortages of raw materials during World War II. The taxation level on strong beers increased almost exponentially as the standard gravity, the baseline from which taxes were calculated, fell from Gladstone's 1.057 (14.2 °P) in 1880 to 1.037 (9.3 °P) in 1950, its final level. But there was further pressure on strong, well-matured beers. The tax was levied on the wort at the time it was pitched to the fermenting vessel, which was also the time when the tax became due! Thus, a high-gravity beer that required several months keeping at the brewery before being shipped to the pub obviously presented the brewer with severe cash-flow problems.

Since the really low beer gravities of the 1940s and 1950s, gravities have recovered slightly. However, the gravity of today's average commercially brewed beer in England is still only just higher than 1 037 (9.3 °P). One bright note is that the timing of the taxation has changed. Since 1993, the tax is now no longer due when the wort is pitched, but only when the beer leaves the brewery gate, and it is based on alcohol content rather than original gravity. As a result, many new microbrewers, as well as some of the bigger regional brewers, have extended their portfolios to include stronger bitters. A good number of these are in the range of 1.050 (12.4 °P) and up, although most are still running beers. However, it is worth pointing out that duty on a pint of beer at 5% alcohol might still be 25 to 35% of the selling price. Drinkers in Britain pay more than half of the total beer duty collected in the European Community![103]

Other events have also played a part in the decline in the strength of English beer. In the early twentieth century, England had a fairly strong prohibitionist, anti–strong drink movement; fortunately, it came to nothing. Since the beginning of the twentieth century, there also has been a trend toward drinking less strong beers and drinking less beer, so overall per capita consumption has fallen from about 40 U.S. gallons in the 1870s to around 30 U.S. gallons per capita in 1990. This trend has accelerated somewhat in recent years because of the public's growing concern over health issues. Another factor in the lowering of beer strength has been increased ownership of cars and hence stringent laws against drinking and driving—people want smaller amounts of weak beer. But as I mentioned earlier in the chapter, I believe the Free

Mash Tun Act was far and away the biggest single influence on the strength of today's beers. I can only wonder what the strength of beers might be if that act had never been passed.

But, why is bitter the predominant style? Why not pale ale? Why not IPA? As I said at the opening of this section, even the concept of what an IPA should be seems to have been forgotten by the few English brewers who still turn out beers under this name. Brewers seemed to use the name pale ale and allowed the name IPA to lapse, just as the East India export trade itself was retrenched. Competition from lagers, as well as outside influences such as Prohibition in America, resulted in the name no longer having the cachet it once had

Bass, the giant of Burton, seemed to have given up the name IPA in favor of pale ale by 1879, as I have already pointed out. It also led a trend towards the term *pale ale* being applied to bottled rather than draught beers. From 1900 to 1905, Bass had 75% of its home trade in bottle; by 1914, 75% of its total pale ale production was sold in bottle.[104] Because of the Bass reputation for quality pale beers, drinkers might have come to consider pale ale a bottled product, while the name bitter stuck to the draught form. In England, there are still some draught beers with the pale ale name. I have found about 30. This compares to about a thousand different draught bitters available in 1997.

The origin of bitter as a style in its own right is much less clear-cut than was the case for IPA. Pale beers dominate today in England, but bitter represents the culmination of a slow trend that started in the eighteenth century. Despite the evident popularity of IPAs in the nineteenth century, the bulk of beers sold then were dark. As porter declined and virtually disappeared in that century, mild ale took over. At first, mild was actually quite a strong beer, often stronger than the porter it was replacing, and usually stronger even than the pale ale offered by the same brewer! According to Charles Graham in "On Lager Beer," Burton Mild had an original gravity of 1.080 (19.3 °P), while the corresponding bitter had an original gravity of 1.064 (15.7 °P) and the pale ale brought up the rear at 1.062 (15.2 °P).[105]

Michael Jackson, in *The New World Guide to Beer*, stated that even as late as the 1940s the term *bitter* might not have been fully established.[106] In some areas, this might be true. For example, mild has always been the beer in England's Industrial Midlands, and the small regional brewer Daniel Batham apparently brewed only dark mild until 1951, when it added a bitter to its regular repertoire. Prior to then, there was apparently no demand for bitter in their tied estate![107] Yet, as far back as 1857, there is a written reference to "Bitter Ale."[108]

Throughout the last quarter of the nineteenth century, there are many references to bitter ales. We have already seen that both bitter and pale ale were brewed in Burton, as well as by other brewers.[109] This suggests that the two were regarded as different styles of beer. Holden's in the Midlands advertised a bitter beer, BB, in 1899.[110] In Newcastle in North-East England, mild is reported to have died out around 1900, while bitter beers (corresponding to the specialty of the Edinburgh brewers), as well as IPAs, had been brewed there several years earlier.[111] Friary, Meux was offering a bitter in 1876, as were other brewers in Guildford, Surrey. Graham also refers to AK Bitter, as well as to Scotch Bitter, in addition to the Burton Bitter. [112]

But why, if bitter was so widespread in the last century, did it not develop a reputation like pale ale did? This is a difficult question to answer. However, it seems to me that this might have been because bitter ales were a little bit of everything to everybody. They included pale ales, as well as beers that were somewhere between pale ales and milds and a whole host of beers under designations such as family pale ale, dinner ale, family ale, light pale ale, and light dinner ale. Much the same applies today, where original gravities of draught bitters range from 1.030 (7.5 °P) to as high as 1.060 (14.7 °P) and encompass a wide range of colors and bitterness.

The rise of bitter ales at first might have marked the brewers' response to customer demands for something lighter than the strong beers that were still the main sellers. Remember that IPAs themselves were not as high in original gravity as the dark Burton ales and porters that they replaced. The AK Bitters, mentioned previously, were closer to modern premium bitters with an original gravity of around 1.045 (11.2 °P). However, it does seem that they were as highly hopped and as well-attenuated as pales and definitely not as sweet as mild ales.

It is also possible that some of the earlier bitter ales were between dark beers and pales in terms of color. Since many of the smaller country brewers were doing their own malting and were not as proficient as the Burton brewers, they might simply have made malts too dark for brewing a pale ale. They might also have had a sense, unlike their modern English counterparts, that pale ale was a clear, well-defined style. Therefore, something that might have been similar, but having not quite the same quality, had to be given a different name. A more cynical possibility is that maybe they were simply adopting the common brewer's technique of using a different name in order to confuse the customer and establish their own brands.

I do not think it was the latter. These beers were definitely highly hopped and very bitter and therefore worthy of their name. I think they were truly a response to what, in retrospect, was a burgeoning demand for a lighter-gravity, lower-alcohol pale beer than had currently been offered. They perhaps did not represent a clear style, and the style really never developed.

Around the turn of the nineteenth century, the range of ingredients available to the brewer became wider, including not just adjuncts, as already discussed, but also a slew of different-colored, different-flavored malts. Brown, pale, amber, and even black patent malt had been available since at least the first quarter of the eighteenth century, even earlier. The brewers could experiment not only with brewing sugars, but also with the crystal malts and malt extracts that had become available since 1880. Perhaps the crystal malts were the most interesting. This was because they could add enticing red color notes to a pale beer, as well as mouth-filling rich caramel tones to its flavor.

Mild ale drinkers who found a straight, highly hopped pale ale too bitter might have been glad to try something that was a little less bitter but still fairly malty. Over a long time, the trend towards pale beers that really started with IPAs eventually resulted in the almost complete elimination of dark beers that appeared first as porters and later became mild ales. It was obviously a trend that was very strong in other countries, such as America, where pale lagers had almost taken over the whole stage even before Prohibition. But the move in England was much slower, with dark draught mild ales still outselling draught bitter in as late as 1960. Pale lagers did not establish any serious position in England until the late 1960s.[113] Charles Graham's prediction that there would be a demand for the lighter, more refreshing lager rather than the heavier English ales of the period would not be quickly fulfilled.[114] Note, however, that the high hopping rates he quoted in "On Lager Beer" are no longer used. Certainly from 1880 on, bittering levels of modern English bitters and pale ales are much lower, in general, than they were in the nineteenth century.

As we have seen, around the turn of the century mild was often stronger than pale or bitter ale. This was to change completely, for reasons that are not very clear. As taxation and other social factors pressed heavily on brewery production costs, the brewers responded by decreasing the original gravities of their beers. Mild suffered the most, perhaps because it (and its predecessor, porter) was favored by working class drinkers. Many of these people were still working in physically demanding jobs such as coal mining and in iron and steel smelting and fabrication, and they consumed a great deal of beer, so price was a strong consideration for them. The paler beers were still favored by the more affluent middle classes, who were probably willing to pay a little extra for them. In addition, such beers still enjoyed the reputation for quality that Burton brewers had created for pale ale.

After World War II, mild from any given brewer was lower in strength than the bitter offered by the same brewer. That situation continues today. Mild has consistently declined in popularity since then, to the extent that many brewers no longer offer a mild and those that do often do so only in a "keg" form, rather than as a traditional real ale. Indeed, the British drinker's consumer group CAMRA (the Campaign for Real Ale) has deemed it necessary to organize a special crusade to save traditional mild ale from extinction.

With the decline of mild in favor of pale beers, bitter became the top-fermented beer that people wanted to drink. A brewer might have only one mild, but he would often have two or more bitters of differing strengths, so he could cater both to the cost-conscious drinker and to his up-market customers. Brewers could—and did—use crystal and other roasted malts (chocolate or black), as well as different hops and hopping rates, to differentiate their bitters from one another and from the products of their competitors.

As the microbrewing renaissance got under way in England in the late 1970s, the trend towards decreasing the original gravity slowed as many of the new brewers saw a market niche in producing stronger than average bitters. In 1997, of the thousand or more real ales under the broad title "bitter," half were in the range 1.040–1.049 (10–12.2 °P) and another 140 were above 1.050 (12.4 °P).[115] In other words, two-thirds of the beers on sale were above the average gravity of about 1.037 (9.3 °P) for all beers sold. If that is not quite clear, the average value is based on the quantities of beer sold at any particular gravity, while the other figures refer to the actual number of brands available. Since the major brewers manufacture on a much larger scale than the micros, it is their outputs that determine the overall average gravity.

But bitter did not have things all its own way. Pale lager was to become a much more important competitor than the declining mild ale. It started to increase in popularity in the early 1960s and continued to gather steam until the 1990s. Today, pale lagers make up almost half of the total English consumption. Many English lagers are of poor quality, low gravity, and high price, sometimes ersatz top-fermented lager rather than the proper bottom-fermented version. Yet many drinkers favor such brews over the traditional beers that are their national heritage.

Much the same could be said of industrial beers of modern America (and those of many other countries!); in fact, even Bud (as it must be called in Britain under copyright laws) and Miller are commonly found in English pubs. Curiously, some Australian beers, which are clearly pale Pilsener-type lagers in style, still bear the name bitter. For example, Castlemaine XXXX is described on its label as a bitter, and a similar brew from Carlton United Breweries bears the name Victoria Bitter. Although such beers are not bitters, this does suggest that the style might have been brewed in Australia earlier in the century, before the widespread move from ales to lagers in that country.

Traditional Real Ale

For the most part, the English drink their beer in pubs, rather than at home. Although this pattern has changed in the last decade or so, it still holds for almost 80% of the beer drunk. This means that most beer is draught beer, rather than bottled or canned. And for centuries that has meant that the pre-eminent English drink has been what is now called *real ale*.

What does that mean? Quite simply, real ale is a living beer. It is racked into a cask after fermentation and undergoes no further processing such as pasteurization, chilling,

Around the corner from the British Museum in London, the Sun offers more real ales than you can swing an empty glass at.

or filtration, although finings and a small amount of priming sugars are often added at racking. The cask is then shipped to the pub, where it undergoes a secondary fermentation in the cellar, thereby giving the beer a suitable carbon dioxide content, or *condition*. So, another term for real ale is *cask-conditioned beer*.

The level of carbon dioxide of these beers is low by American standards. I discuss just how low in chapter 4. But because the beer is made with top-fermenting yeast and must referment in the cask, it cannot be kept very cold. Such yeasts cannot work well below about 52 °F (11 °C), which is about the lowest temperature likely to be reached in a good cellar in the English climate. So such beers are at their best when served at 52–55 °F (11–13 °C).

Further, they are served from the cask either by gravity or by mechanical means, with air allowed to enter the cask as the beer is drawn off. Such beer must not be propelled from the cask by carbon dioxide, or it is not real ale. However, air can cause problems, not only with oxidation, but also by permitting the entry of souring organisms such as lactobacilli and acetic bacteria. Thus, handling cask-conditioned beer is a difficult art. When done properly, however, the result is a beer of unique character and flavor and one found hardly anywhere else in the world today.

Let me point out, for the sake of the argument that follows, that in terms of real ale there is a very important difference between a cask and a keg. A cask has two holes—one to take a tap from which the beer is dispensed and one to permit gas to escape during conditioning and to let air in during dispense. An English keg has only one hole. A hollow spear is inserted into this hole, and carbon dioxide or mixed pressure is used to force the beer out through the spear. Such kegs do not permit natural conditioning of the beer, as there is no vent for carbon dioxide to escape. They are designed to handle pasteurized beers, which have higher carbon dioxide levels than do cask-conditioned beers.

To return to history, I earlier alluded to the fact that English brewers around the end of the nineteenth century moved to acquire and "tie" pubs to their products in what was called the *tied-house system*. This went to such an extent that only a small number of pubs remained that were not owned by breweries. The corollary of that is that after the turn of the century, the best way for a brewing company to acquire new outlets was to buy up other brewers and then close down the brewing operations of the new purchase and put their beer into the newly bought pubs.

A central theme of capitalism in our times is the tendency of companies to grow through amalgamation. For English brewing, the tied-house system added an extra edge to this philosophy, and throughout the twentieth century there has been an ever-greater concentration of pubs in the hands of a few, large brewing companies. By the late 1960s, these companies had become what were dubbed the "Big Six": Allied Breweries, Bass, Courage, Scottish and Newcastle, Watney's, and Whitbread. Combined, they controlled over 70% of the pubs in England and between them had almost a monopoly in the brewing industry in that they could dictate what was sold to the customer and therefore what kind of beer he would drink.

The principal problem with the Big Six was their attempt to boot out real ale and to force on the public keg bitter and mild. This meant that a chilled, filtered, pasteurized beer was put into a keg and then dispensed by carbon dioxide pressure. The result was a bland, gassy, characterless beer that could be sold only by means of heavy expenditure on advertising, usually at the expense of any publicity for the same company's real ale. Watney's was the first to experiment with this kind of beer, way back in the 1930s, but it was not until the late 1950s that it began to push keg Red Barrel. Whitbread soon followed with its Flowers brand, and the other four quickly jumped on the bandwagon. For a while, it looked as though traditional real ale was doomed, as its share of the market continued to shrink.

Although some of the smaller regional breweries gave in and began producing keg beer, others held out and continued to make real ale. One of the holdouts was Young's of South London, which actually made a sales point of its insistence on brewing real ale. Of course, I could be biased in their favor, as I lived within a mile of the brewery for many years, and Young's was the first beer I ever drank. It also transpires that the first brewer on the site of Young's Ram Brewery in Wandsworth back in the sixteenth century had the same name as my mother's family.[116] While not a common name, as yet I have not established that there is any direct link.

The point of all this is that in 1970, CAMRA was formed as a protest against the advancement of keg beers at the expense of real ale. At first, it consisted of just a few people who were aware that the quality of English beer was deteriorating and who wanted to do something about that. But many other drinkers felt the same way, and soon CAMRA burgeoned into what has been called *the* most successful consumer campaign ever (notwithstanding America's Ralph Nader). Even the big brewers had to listen. As a result, real ale became the flavor of the month, with almost every pub stocking at least one version and some offering a huge variety. The regionals prospered, and the new microbrewing movement started. Between 1972 and 1997, more than 350 operating breweries opened.[117] Even the Big Six moved away from keg beer and back to the traditional style brew. And everybody lived happily ever after.

We wish! I already pointed out that pale lager had taken a huge amount of the English market, pushing out bitter and mild. Further turmoil was to come. As a result of the Monopolies and Mergers Commission on Beer Supply in England, the 1989 Beer Orders were passed, limiting pub ownership in order to prevent a few breweries from controlling the market. Ironically, one result of this was that Watney's gave up brewing altogether to concentrate on pub ownership; their Mortlake, Surrey, brewery now produces only Bud. Courage took over supplying Watney's pubs with beer and then themselves were taken over by Scottish and Newcastle. In 1997, Bass tried to take over Carlsberg-Tetley (which had come out of Allied Breweries), but fortunately was forestalled by Prime Minister Tony Blair's New Labour Government.

As the bigger breweries sold off pubs, several large pub-owning companies formed. These have had the power to force large discounts from their suppliers, which have inevitably been the large companies, rather than regional or craftbrewers. Indeed, even some of the regionals have turned themselves into pub-owning companies, either selling or spinning off their breweries. Included among these are Boddington's of Manchester; Eldridge, Pope of Dorchester (brewers of the famous vintage beer Thomas Hardy Ale); and Gibbs, Mew of Salisbury in Wiltshire.

Another provision coming out of the 1989 Beer Orders was the so-called "guest beer." According to this provision, any publican tied to a brewer had the right to stock a guest beer of his choice from *any* other supplier. It was designed to limit the monopoly of the tied system and to encourage small and craftbrewers. Although it has been partially successful, it has been limited in its effect on microbrewers. This is because the major companies, as well as the newer pub-owning chains, developed a short list of approved guest beer suppliers. Their publicans were forced to choose from this list, rather

The Gibbs, Mew brewery tap is just a short walk from the Salisbury Cathedral.
Sadly, this picture was taken a few months before the brewery closed.

than going out to the open market. How all this upheaval will turn out in the end is still not clear. If the majors should move to get out of brewing and become only pub owners, as some brewing analysts predict, the English brewing scene could, early in the next century, turn out similar to the American model, with a very small number of brewers dominating the market with essentially the same product.

Although the lifeless keg beer of the 1960s and 1970s has been largely forgotten, a new enemy to real ale has emerged—the nitrokeg. Guinness pioneered the use of nitrogen and carbon dioxide mixtures for dispensing its draught version. In the early 1990s, other companies adapted it for dispensing processed bitter (that is, chilled, filtered, pasteurized, and carbonated keg, canned, and even bottled beers). Nitrokeg is a method of dispensing in which mixed-gas dispense gives a beer with a low carbon dioxide content that is smooth-drinking, like a real ale, but still stable and much easier to handle than traditional real ale. Some beers of this type are available in cans in America, usually with the word *pub* somewhere in their name to impress the unwary drinker with the idea that he is getting something every bit as good as real ale. CAMRA disagrees strongly with this practice and is fighting hard to prevent it from further pushing out real ale. But it will be a struggle, for the new-style smooth beers have proven to be quite successful and are being heavily publicized by the big brewers (who seldom spend any significant money on advertising real ale). It might be that mixed-gas dispense is not, itself, a bad thing and detracts only a little from a well-made beer. The problem really lies in the fact that it is applied to processed, bland, and characterless beers. Carefully brewed traditional bitter, properly kept and conditioned in cask and then mechanically dispensed, is unquestionably English beer at its best. Real ale is still king to any drinker who wants beer with character and flavor.

America and IPA

I have left the subject of America and IPA until last because the history of pale ales is largely an English one. But it is not the least section, because modern American microbrewers, unlike their English counterparts, have remained much truer to the original IPA.

English-style ales were brewed in America almost since the landing of the *Mayflower*, although only on a very small scale until the latter part of the eighteenth century. As industrialization got under way, so too did commercial brewing. But the American eighteenth-century brewers (largely concentrated in Philadelphia and New York City) seem to have focused on brewing porter, brown ales, and even some mild ales. Pale ale did not fit into the picture, and it remained small-scale compared to what was going on in England. For example, in 1810 there were 132 commercial brewers in America. Their total production was 185,000 barrels, compared to 235,100 barrels turned out in the same year by *just one* London brewer—Barclay, Perkins.[118]

The American brewing industry was still small when the lager revolution began. For example, steam engines were not widely used until around the 1850s, almost 70 years after the London porter brewers had found it necessary to mechanize. Lager yeast was first brought to American by John Wagner, a Philadelphia brewer, probably around 1840. After that, pale lager beers rapidly established themselves, helped by the high level of German immigration around that time. At first, lager brewing was a very local affair, its product designed for consumption by a population close by. But it soon became more popular, perhaps helped by the hot climates of the new areas of the country that were being opened up to settlers.

Thus, lager was on the scene in America about the time pale ale brewing began. This meant that pale ale never established the market share that it did in England, where lager did not become significantly popular until after World War II. As a result, nothing like the development of pale ale into bitter ever occurred in America. Indeed, until recently, nothing like bitter was being produced in the United States, and only a few beers were brewed that were true top-fermented pale, bitter ales. That changed dramatically with the arrival of the microbrewing revolution, but I get to that a little later.

When I came to America in 1977, domestic beers were almost entirely pale lagers, only very loosely in the Pilsener style. Homebrewing remained illegal, although it was still carried on clandestinely. The more sophisticated drinkers protested this situation by purchasing ever-increasing amounts of more distinctive imported beers. When I first arrived, I was dreadfully disappointed in what was offered at my local liquor stores. One exception was Ballantine's IPA, brewed at that time in Narragansett, Rhode Island. Intrigued by the label, I tried it, not really expecting too much. What a surprise! It was full of malty body, stuffed with hop character and bitterness, and over-laid with the flavor of oak—something entirely new to me in a beer. I decided that all was not lost if I could drink beer like that!

Peter Ballantine, a Scot, moved to America around 1833 and set up a brewery in Albany, New York, then an important brewing center.[119] In 1840, he moved to Newark, New Jersey, and started brewing there. It is not clear when he first produced his IPA, but at the time that he moved, Burton IPA was in its first flowering in England. Perhaps, just as the German immigrants took their own lager methods with them, so did Ballantine take with him the IPA he loved. He also brewed a Ballantine Ale, which was likewise produced in Rhode Island when I came to

America. However, it was more like a pale, lightly hopped bitter than an IPA. He also brewed Burton Ale, reportedly aged for up to ten years. I have not found an example of this beer myself, but according to Michael Jackson in his *Brewer's Guardian* article—"Will the Americans help us discover our IPA heritage?"—it also was a pale beer, rather than of the dark Burton style.[120]

It is interesting to note that Ballantine's IPA was one of the handful of beers that survived Prohibition (as did Ballantine's Ale). It also outlived a series of takeovers of the brewery, first in Newark and then when the Falstaff group bought the Newark brewery, after which its production was moved to Rhode Island, then to Fort Wayne, Indiana, and finally to its present site in Milwaukee, Wisconsin. Ballantine's IPA was dry-hopped, using whole hops, and given hop character by means of hop oil produced by the brewery's own steam-distillation process. As late as the 1960s, it had 60 IBU, thereby making it very bitter by modern standards.

Ballantine's IPA apparently was matured for a year in oak tanks, accounting for its unusual caky flavor. Where Ballantine got this idea is unknown, and this flavor was certainly not matched in any English IPA. Maybe he used American oak vessels because he had no access to European oak and then found that he liked the flavor obtained from the more porous American wood. Did he consider an oak flavor to be an authentic characteristic of IPA? If so, was he actually correct in this view or had he simply assumed it to be the case because the early IPAs spent so much time in oak casks? Clearly, the English IPA did not pick up any flavors from the wood. There also is some evidence that at least a few of the brewers lined their casks with pitch.[121] This was probably done to ensure the integrity of the cask, rather than to prevent the beer from developing a wood flavor, but the effect on flavor would have been the same.

I have talked with one or two English coopers about this. They were emphatic that the density of the wood would not permit the leaching of oak flavors into the beer. My own experience drinking real ale from wooden casks, which were the norm for beer storage in England when I first began drinking beer, is that English bitter beers had no oak character whatsoever. However, since these would have been running beers—stored in casks for only a week or two—it's possible there simply was not enough time to pick up such flavors. Perhaps more to the point, casks were used and reused many times, with quite severe steam cleaning between each use. This certainly would have leached out tannins, vanillins, and any other beer-soluble oak chemicals. Yet, just for the record,

Pamela Sambrook, in her book *Country House Brewing in England*, reports that in the great country house breweries of the seventeenth and eighteenth centuries, it was customary to treat new wooden casks before use.[122] Such treatment included scalding with boiling mixtures of grain, walnut leaves, and new hay or straw and then storing the casks for a week or more before use. She goes on to say that new casks were used for *small beer only for the first year!* Of course, such treatments might have been simply to ensure that the casks were clean and watertight. They might not have been top-grade oak casks like those favored by the Burton brewers and might even have been made of other woods.

The modern version of Ballantine IPA no longer has the complexity of hop bitterness, hop character, and oakiness of the original, but it still remains an interesting brew. Other American ales produced in the late eighteenth and early nineteenth centuries were pale in color and very bitter, but these were generally called stock ales, rather than IPAs or pale ales. Stock ales were brewed only from pale malt, with additions of 25% sugar in the grist. Original gravities were around 1.064–1.072 (15.7– 17.5 °P), and hop rates were high, as much as 2–3 pounds/barrel (5–8 ounces per 5 U.S. gallons), which would certainly have put them into the IPA range.[123] It is not clear how common these ales were. Probably they were rare, since at that time ales in general were on the decline in America.

Very few American ales survived the trauma of Prohibition and of those that did, many were converted to the bastard cream ale style. These are mostly bottom-fermented beers, very pale in color and not very bitter. Nor, in my opinion, are they very much different from the ubiquitous American industrial Pilseners. And there, for a while, the story rested, with only Ballantine's IPA remaining as a tenuous link with English pale ales and bitters.

The story took a new turn with the revival of steam beer by Fritz Maytag in his San Francisco Anchor Brewery. This beer, although bottom fermented, can be regarded as a subspecies of bitter/pale ale in that it is a pale, noticeably bitter beer with some ale-type fruitiness, rather than the "smoother" lager flavor. Maytag was intrigued by Ballantine's Burton Ale and subsequently visited several English traditional breweries.[124] There he was further intrigued by the use of dry-hopping in cask, which in turn led to his introducing Liberty Ale in 1975, a dry-hopped pale beer of 1.057 OG (14 °P). Although considered by many to be an IPA, Liberty Ale actually represented a new style of the beer. This was because it was aggressively hopped with American Cascades, which gave the beer a very distinctive, floral character.

I remember tasting this in front of a group of enthusiastic New England homebrewers in the early 1980s and remarking, "They could bury me with a cask of this!"

Liberty Ale could be regarded as simply carrying on the Burton tradition—recall that Bass used considerable amounts of American hops in the nineteenth and twentieth centuries. However, these hops would have been mainly from the East Coast, probably New York (as would those Ballantine used originally). Also, they probably would have been more like English hops, such as Northern Brewer and Bramling Cross, although as I said earlier in the chapter, their black currant flavor was not English. They would almost certainly not have been anything like Cascades, which was not developed and grown in the American Northwest until well into this century.

It is the use of American hops, and Cascades in particular, that defines the new American IPA style, even though many such beers are truer to the original than modern English beers under that name. American IPA has become a style all its own, or at least a substyle of pale ale, for Liberty Ale was followed by others in a similar vein.

In 1981, brewer Bert Grant took a step in a different direction, with an IPA from Yakima Brewing Company. This beer supposedly was based on historical data and brewed in the style of an original IPA. With about 60 IBU (from American hops), it certainly had the bitterness required for the style, but its original gravity of 1.048 (11.9 °P) was somewhat low for an "original" pale ale. It can be argued that Grant broke new ground by introducing the modern American drinker to very bitter beers and in doing so really started the whole trend to such beers, particularly in the Northwest states.

Also in 1981 came the founding of the Sierra Nevada Brewing Company and the subsequent production of its pale ale. To me, this ale is perhaps the defining pale ale of the new American style. It is somewhat low in original gravity, 1.052 (12.9 °P), and is brewed with a yeast that gives it a very clean characteristic with little of the estery fruitiness so typical of an ale. The lower original gravity and lack of ester character did not fit the specifications of the original English IPAs, but its hoppiness certainly did. The really distinguishing characteristic of this beer was the brewer's liberal use of Cascades, both for hop bitterness and hop character. The floral, herbal nature of this hop seems to burst out of this beer at every angle, making it both big and complex and far removed from anything offered by mainstream American brewers.

As the microbrewing movement flourished in America, others followed the IPA trend. Pike Brewing Company (Seattle), Harpoon Brewery (Boston), Steelhead Brewery

(Eugene, Oregon), the now-defunct Manhattan Brewery (New York), Shipyard Brewing (Portland, Maine), and several others have produced IPAs. Not all used Cascades, but all used American hops. This generally resulted in beers of more powerful hop character than could be achieved with the traditional English pale ale varieties, Goldings and Fuggles. Given the decline of IPA in England, this is a very important development. American microbrewers can be proud of their efforts not only in bringing back a historically important beer style, but also in taking it a step further and giving it an undeniably American character.

However, there was another important occurrence in American microbrewing. Most of the new American micros that sprang up concentrated on ale production. This is a somewhat simpler process than lager production, and, perhaps more important, it requires a good deal less space and capital, so it lent itself well to small companies starting up on a low budget. There was a lead-in from England, too, where microbrewing got under way rather earlier—in the 1970s—producing, of course, mainly ales. A good number of these American micros got their start with equipment designed by supply companies originally set up to cater to the English market. A notable example of this was Peter Austin, who started out by setting up the Ringwood brewery in Hampshire.

Many of the new micros offered versions of pale ale, those generally tending towards somewhat higher gravities than the English average. In addition, some brewed versions of extra special bitter (ESB), seeing this as a style in itself. It is not. Rather, it is really only a bitter at the top end of the original gravity range. Although there are comparable beers in England, I know of only one that is actually called an ESB, which is brewed by Fuller's in London (although there are a fair number of beers brewed in England at similar gravities to Fuller's ESB). Even this beer was only introduced in the 1970s! It was actually first sold as a winter ale, replacing, of all things, Fuller's dark Old Burton![125]

Other American micros turned out something they called *amber ale*. One example was Newman's Albany Amber Ale, produced at Newman's in Albany, New York, the first American microbrewery I visited. On the East Coast, New Amsterdam Amber was available early on and was contract-brewed for a New York company; Catamount Amber out of Vermont soon followed. However, Mendocino's Red Tail Ale, introduced in 1983, might be the first example of an amber ale. This appellation became fairly common all over the country, and some have argued that it should be treated as a separate style.[126] It is usually a somewhat darker beer than pale ale, relying on crystal malts to differentiate it from pale ale, and it is generally not aggressively hopped. It was a wide-ranging style at first. Some examples of it were quite big and malty and even quite bitter, while others were much more restrained. Some brewers even looked upon it as a stepping stone between mainstream lagers and the more characterful pale ales, intending it to introduce inquiring but less sophisticated drinkers to beers of character.

It could be argued that American amber ale fits nicely into the wide-ranging English bitter style. One American microbrewer was quoted as saying that such ales were regarded as bitters, but no micro in America wanted to use that name for fear of offending potential customers! Their amber color is certainly no darker than that of many modern English bitters. Also, most English brewers use caramel or crystal malts in their bitters. Amber ales are usually all-malt beers, with no adjuncts, but this does not in itself distinguish them from bitters. Although the use of sugar and adjuncts is common English practice, many of the new English micros use only malt.

Amber ales differ somewhat from English bitter. They are usually brewed with domestic malt and hops, and the lighter character of domestic pale malts leads to a greater emphasis on crystal malt flavors. However, perhaps the most important difference between the two types of beer is that American amber ales are not normally real ales.

This is because they are served at much higher carbonation levels than true cask-conditioned beer. Also, they are usually filtered, although many of them are sterile-filtered so as to avoid the need for pasteurization. I return to this issue in chapter 2. But I point out here that these last two factors would be enough for any English devotee of traditional beers to argue that American amber ales have a quite different character and flavor from a true real ale.

A most intriguing later development in the American microbrewing scene is that even cask-conditioned real ale is now being brewed. A number of brewpubs have offered something called real ale for quite a while, when they have served straight from the conditioning tanks to the bar. However, although this ale has not been filtered, all too often it has been kept under a carbon dioxide blanket, thereby resulting in a much gassier product than real ale should be. CAMRA's definition of real ale explicitly excludes the introduction of carbon dioxide, either as a protective blanket or for dispense.

Genuine real ale currently is available only in America on a relatively small scale and in limited quantities from a few brewers, such as Wharf Rat in Baltimore; the Sherlock's Home in Minnetonka, Minnesota; and Atlantic Coast Brewing in Boston. There have even been a couple of real ale symposiums held in Chicago. At the 1997 one, at least 100 American-brewed real ales were offered, although fewer than half of those were pale beers. It is intriguing to wonder just how popular this type of ale will become in the United States. It likely will remain a very small part of pub and microbrewery sales, which in itself is only a niche market.

American microbrewing is a vibrant and growing industry, and no one knows how big it will eventually become. Already there are more new micros and brew-pubs in the United States than there are in England, although they are, of course, much more spread out. The brewing industry has come a long way in the 20 years I have lived in America, and good beer is no longer almost impossible to find. But we are still a long way from having a good pub on the corner of every street. There are none in my town, although there are some good micros within reasonable traveling distance, with more and more coming on the scene each year.

One thing is sure—the art of brewing pale ale is just as alive and well in America as it is in its original home, England. And in many ways, the American small brewer has been more inventive than his English counterpart, giving the pale ale style a greater depth and dimension than it ever had.

Chapter 2

Style Definitions
and Profiles
of Pale Ales

Brewers who want to follow their own individual path can ignore styles if they wish and still produce perfectly good beers. But I want to explain here why the concept of style is both necessary and useful. I also want to define the attributes of the pale ale style and the substyles that make up this great class of beer. My reasons for doing this are quite simple: You just cannot brew pale ale, or beer of any particular style, unless you understand what the attributes of that style are.

Why Do We Need Style Definitions?

For all of the important input of new American brewers, pale ale is still an English style. Yet, pale ale is not the correct title for the style! In modern terms, most English beers are bitters, and brews such as pale ale, IPA, light ale, American IPA, amber ale, and so on are really substyles of the great class of bitter. In using the term *pale ale*, we bow to the historical derivation of this beer. Yet, even this is wrong. As I mentioned in chapter 1, IPA was the precursor of pale ales, so history says we should really use the term *IPA* to include all of these other beers.

But all of this is semantics. Perhaps you feel that it is unnecessary jargon, that there is really no need to define a style and that all that matters is whether the beer in question tastes good. In this respect, it is interesting to look at what might be regarded as the classic books on brewing technology. Few of these attempt to define styles, and generally they deal with them in a very cursory manner. For example, H. Lloyd Hind, in *Brewing Science and Practice*, does not mention bitter at all.[1] However, he does quote two pale ales at original gravities of 1.055 (13.6 °P) and 1.050 (12.4 °P) and a "light pale ale for bottling" at the lower gravity of 1.040 (10.0 °P). The revered brewing scientist Jean de Clerck, in *A Textbook of Brewing*, refers only to pale ale, or bitter, and makes no distinction between the two.[2]

A more modern English text, *Malting and Brewing Science, Volume I*, published in 1971, refers just briefly to pale ales when discussing beer types and gives only a bitter recipe when it comes to grist preparation.[3] More recent American books are no better. William Hardwick says in 1995's *Handbook of Brewing*, "Pale ale is also called bitter,"[4] while the German writer, W. Kunze, differentiates in *Technology Brewing and Malting* between them by stating that bitter is a darker beer than is pale ale.[5] Further, a duo of American and English brewing gurus, Michael J. Lewis and Tom W. Young, make no mention of the styles at all in their book, *Brewing!*[6]

I am not sure what all this means. Perhaps it reflects the fact that the writers simply find it almost impossible to define styles or that today's brewing scientists are concentrating too much on the brewing process at the expense of beers of character. More likely, they would say that all that matters is good beer and that the concept of style in itself is unnecessary. So why do we want to talk in terms of a style and to try to define what a beer should be like in order to fit its designated style?

There are some fairly obvious reasons for pinning down beer styles. For example, homebrewing competitions would be chaotic without any guidelines to follow. You can compare 10 or so very different beers, as is done in the best of show category, but you cannot compare stouts directly with IPAs or barley wines or Pilseners or Belgian ales when you are dealing with hundreds, or even thousands, of entries. A second reason is that the idea of a distinct style is very convenient shorthand for beer writers and their readers. For example, without the idea of a style, it would be very difficult for me to recommend a particular beer or even a pub and its products and to have you understand what is really good about it and decide whether you want to seek it out for yourself. Rather than simply saying how well it matches the style, I would have to describe in great detail how every beer is brewed in order to give you an idea what it was like.

Third, the idea of what a certain style should be is very useful to brewers, whether amateur or professional. A good yardstick of your brewing ability is how well your brew matches what you set out to achieve, as defined by style guidelines. In addition, an able brewer should be able to devise a suitable recipe by interpreting the attributes of a particular style. The concept is useful even for beginners, since kit manufacturers, for example, usually use style designations to sell their products.

Fourth, it is important that you drink beer with an understanding of what a style should be in order to develop a taste for the various aspects of beer flavor. How can you judge whether you really like a beer unless you comprehend why it tastes like it does? If you don't know what hop bitterness is, how can you say whether you like the bitterness in the beer you are drinking or whether you want something with a more malty character? If you cannot make that kind of distinction, what kind of criteria can you possibly use to distinguish between good and bad beers?

Fifth, we need style definitions in order to pay proper homage to beer's long history. While Henry Ford said that history is bunk and we should certainly not be slaves to it, it also is true that only an idiot would ignore lessons that have already been learned. The wise brewer draws on the lessons of history in the light of modern scientific knowledge of the brewing process. This is particularly important for microbrewers that, rather than merely copying modern industrial beers, want to produce a beer of character, one that is true to its heritage and yet can be handled and distributed in a modern context.

Perhaps the most important reason for being concerned about style definitions is that it is a way to keep commercial brewers honest. Unfortunately, such brewers have, in their rush to sell their products, too often proved eager to give their beers appellations and heritage that they do not merit. I mentioned in chapter 1 how the term IPA has been applied to beers in England that clearly do not bear any relationship to the original IPA. British brewers, too, have tried hard to persuade drinkers that low-gravity, top-fermented, adjunct-laden lagers are every bit as good as anything out of Germany. They also have tried to pass off filtered, pasteurized keg beers as being the same as traditional cask-conditioned brews. The big American brewers are already moving in on the microbrewing scene. In some cases, they are tied up with micros in distribution deals and partnerships, while in others, they introduce "specialty" beers of their own—even Anheuser-Busch has come out with a pale ale.

And of course, the world is awash with beers called "Pils" or "Pilsener," none of which bear any resemblance to the creations of the town of Pilsen. Homebrewing books commonly state that it is difficult to brew American light beers because there are no strong flavors to hide brewing faults. What kind of a beer is it when that is the only positive thing you can say about it?

Commercial imperatives mean that big brewers will always tend to blur style definitions. They do not really understand the individual brew of character that will appeal only to a minority of drinkers. Like so many other manufacturers, they have become obsessed with the "brand" concept. And let me be quite clear that this concept is aimed at getting consumers to buy by name and not by the quality they perceive in the product.

How does a drinker know what qualities to look for in a beer? By tasting it, of course. Ideally, the drinker will be expert enough to rate, by taste alone, any beer as worthwhile or not. More likely, they will start by choosing a style and assessing whether the beer is good within the limits of that style. Defining a style is a question of setting standards, and quality is all about standards and principles.

This does not mean that style definitions must be limiting. They are guidelines only. To quote one writer, "Style guidelines ought to be descriptive, not prescriptive."[7] Brewers making a pale ale should work within certain limits, if their product is to be authentic. Yet, they might deviate from some of those in order to improve their product and even to invent a new style or substyle of an existing style. Deviating from all of them might result in the "ultimate beer," but please, do not call it a pale ale! What is also unacceptable is deviating from the style limits in order to cheapen the beer or to dumb it down just to appeal to a larger audience, and then draw on the style's heritage as a selling point.

For further interesting discussions on the need for style definitions, read "The Last Wort" by Alan Moen and "Beer Styles: An International Analysis" by Keith Thomas.[8]

Sorting Out What Makes a Style—Bitter Rules!

In my youth, I thought differentiating among styles was simple: pale ale was bottled, and bitter was draught. In the first edition of *Pale Ale*, I gaily simplified things and made a quite arbitrary split between pale ale, bitter, and IPA based on original gravity. Later, I realized the situation was more complex than that, and now I see the whole issue as incredibly complicated! Not only is there pale ale, light ale, IPA, bitter, ESB, American amber ale, American pale ale, and American IPA, but also cask-conditioned bitters, filtered and pasteurized keg versions, beers served with carbon dioxide pressure or mixed nitrogen/carbon dioxide, and micro-filtered beers. Even bottled beers can be filtered and pasteurized, sterile filtered, or bottle-conditioned. I realized that all of these different methods of packaging and serving the beer can have just as profound an effect on its flavor as the techniques used in the actual brewing process.

It could be argued also that beers from other countries might be included under the pale ale banner. *Kölsch* beer from Cologne, Germany, and some of the strong Belgian ales could be considered to belong to this category, but they actually are different enough to be considered styles in their own right. I discussed in the last chapter how the Scots played a significant part in the history of pale ale. However, true Scottish ales are in a category of their own. This is because they emphasize malt rather than hops, and hoppiness is a dominant factor in pale ales. Some very good bitters and pale ales are brewed in Scotland and in Wales today, but these are generally in the style that originated in England.

To make some sense of this category, I start with English bitters. I made a survey of them from several published sources.[9] They include both bottled and draught beers. Some of the former are filtered and pasteurized, and others are conditioned in the bottle. All of the draught beers are cask-conditioned, that is, they are not filtered and pasteurized keg beers; those dispensed by mixed gas are excluded. These latter largely represent the output of the major brewers, which almost by definition is brewed to average

An idyllic English village and an oddly named inn with a brewery attached–what more could you want?

specifications and can be ignored for our purposes—perhaps an arbitrary decision, but at best such beers can be regarded only as a lesser variation of the style.

The survey, whose results are summarized in figure 1, showed that of 1,187 beers, 1,043 are draught and only 144 (12%) are bottled. Of the 1,187, 41 (3.5%) are designated as IPAs and 82 (6.9%) as pale and light ales. Thus, bitters total 1,064 (89.6%), and even among bottled beers, 58% of them are designated as bitter!

FIGURE 1

Occurrence of English Pale Ale Varieties

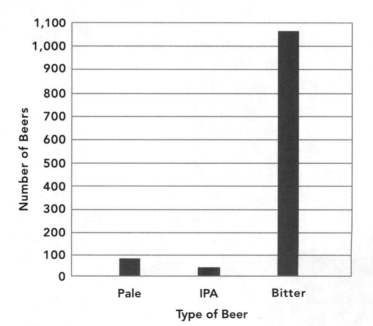

This survey shows fairly conclusively the dominance of draught bitter among English beers. In fact, the "bitter" column heading in figure 1 represents the three major categories as determined by original gravity: 1.030–1.039 (7.6–9.8 °P), 1.040–1.049 (10.0–12.2 °P), and 1.050+ (12.4 °P+). These can be broadly described as, respectively, ordinary bitter, best bitter, and strong bitter. However, those are really marketing terms, and they are confusing in that they are only relative. Some brewers offer beers in each of these ranges, some have more than one in any or even all of the ranges, others

FIGURE 2

Distribution of Bitter Ales

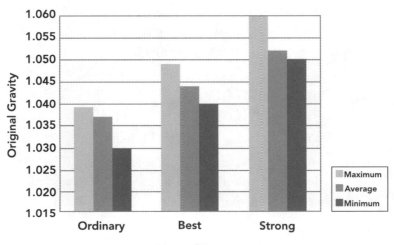

have beers in any two of the three, and a few offer only one. Figure 1 does not quite tell the whole story, since it shows only the total number of bitters. A better picture can be obtained by looking at the average for each range, as shown in figure 2.

In the figure, the center bar of each trio is the average for each category:

Ordinary	1.037 (9.3 °P)
Best	1.044 (11.0 °P)
Strong	1.052 (12.9 °P)

Clearly, there is some skew in these numbers, with ordinary coming close to the top of its range, best in the lower half, and strong only just over its lowest limit. In fact, the American Homebrewers Association (AHA) 1998 Competition Style Guidelines Chart actually fits these averages quite nicely, giving the following ranges: [10]

Ordinary	1.033–1.038 (8.2–9.5 °P)
Best	1.038–1.045 (9.5–11.3 °P)
Strong	1.045–1.060 (11.5–15.0 °P)

I prefer the wider ranges for the three designations. But where does that leave English pale ale? The AHA designates it as being 1.044–1.056 (11.0–13.8 °P); in other words, it spans the top of the range for best bitter into the bottom of that for strong bitter. Michael Jackson states in *The New World Guide to Beer* that a premium gravity bitter might sometimes be designated as pale ale.[11] But, as I showed earlier in the chapter, less than 7% of English cask-conditioned beer and bottled beer is actually called pale ale by their brewers! In fact, of the beers I surveyed the total number of draught and bottled pale and light ales ran to only 52, with an average gravity of 1.034 (8.5 °P) and a range of 1.026–1.056 (6.6–13.8 °P). Note that light ales are low-gravity bottled beers and are often simply bottled versions of a draught bitter (they are invariably chilled, filtered, carbonated, and pasteurized). For our purposes here, they can hardly be regarded as classic beers, and since their inclusion in the style only further confuses some pretty complex relationships, I propose to ignore them from now on in this book.

Some bottled pale ales fit Michael Jackson's designation, notably Worthington White Shield at 1.056 (13.8 °P); its pedigree extends back to the original IPAs. Bass brewed this beer after absorbing Worthington's Brewing. Now they have licensed its production to the regional brewer King & Barnes of Sussex.[12] Another in this category, at least for someone with my predilections, is Young's Ramrod at 1.049 (12.2 °P), a beer available in America.

I agree with Michael Jackson that English pale ales are bottled beers, with gravities of 1.045–1.055 (11.2–13.6 °P). In modern terms, these are mainly processed beers, rather than bottle-conditioned. However, commercially brewed bottle-conditioned beers have undergone something of a renaissance in England in the last few years. This is the same gravity range I quoted in the first edition of *Pale Ale* and is clearly arbitrary. Given that most beers now called "pale ale" are of a much lower original gravity than this, it is clear that in this case I am defining pale ale on the basis of what it should be, rather than what it is!

Note that this original gravity puts pale ale in the same gravity band as strong bitters. But since these are draught beers, there will be some flavor differences between them and bottled pale ale. Pale ale is sometimes described as having a nuttier flavor than draught bitter. It will certainly have a more "prickly" character due to the higher carbonation in bottle (even if it is bottle-conditioned and not pasteurized). To some extent, it also will be drier than cask-conditioned bitter and might therefore appear to be somewhat more bitter. In addition, cask-conditioned bitters might be dry hopped in the cask, thereby giving it a hop aroma and character that is not present in bottled beers. Dry hopping in England is sometimes considered a common practice with cask-conditioned beers (see, for example, Michael Jackson).[13] It seems to me that many modern English bitters do not have much in the way of dry-hop character, and certainly they have less than they did 20 or more years ago. Or is it just that everybody says, as they get older, that "beer isn't what it was"?

ESB-type bitters fall into the class of strong draught bitter, although the original ESB from Fuller's is also sold in bottle. However, unlike some American brewers, I do not see this as a separate substyle. I see it more as a brand name for a particular strong bitter and do not propose to call it anything else.

When it comes to bittering levels and color, there is a good deal less information available on English bitter. What there is shows that there is little difference in bitterness levels between the three draught types. They all fall into the range of 21–45 IBU, and it is surprising that there is no clear-cut pattern of increasing bittering with increasing beer strength. This would indicate that ordinary bitters frequently might taste more bitter than their stronger, more malty relatives. It might also indicate that some brewers underhop a beer that, by definition, should be bitter. However, I have bittering data on only about 15% of the total number of beers in the survey, so the sample is rather small to make firm conclusions. Note that this gives a very different picture than that given in the AHA style guidelines, which quote IBUs of 20–35 for ordinary bitter, 28–46 for best bitter, and 30–55 for strong bitter.[14] While this order of increasing bitterness with increasing strength is what I would favor in my own brewing, it does not reflect the reality of the English market. It would mean that, for example, Draught Bass at an original gravity of 1.043 (10.7 °P) and 26 IBU would not fit the AHA guidelines for IPA.[15]

As for color, I have data on an even smaller sample—about 10% of the total. The range of these is surprisingly wide, 5–26 °SRM, with the average being 13 °SRM. This is certainly wider than the 8–14 °SRM I quoted in my first book (this figure is also what is given in the AHA style guidelines). This represents in part a trend in England to brew "summer" beers. These are generally supposed to be more thirst-quenching than bitters and are pale enough that they usually have "gold" or "golden" in their brand name. Such beers are brewed with only very lightly roasted crystal malt, or even none at all—this is what makes them so pale. Although this practice is often represented as being a new development, there have been bitters around for years that have a pale straw or golden color. These are probably more common in the North of

England than elsewhere. I remember my first encounter with Theakston's Best Bitter (when it was still brewed by a Theakston!) and how pale it appeared to me. Boddington's was also quite pale by bitter standards, at least in the days when it was a regional brew.

In general terms, bitters can be anything from pale gold to a deep copper-red. The darker colors result from the use of high-roasted crystal malts or from very small additions of chocolate or black malts. These add not only color, but also complexity to the flavor, and they are favored by many brewers on this account. Some cynics would say that these malts are used to hide the fact that hop rates have been decreased and the beers are not as bitter as they should be. That is certainly not generally the case with cask-conditioned beers, but it might well have been practiced with certain national brands of keg bitter.

India Pale Ales

English IPAs, in the modern sense, are much harder to define, simply because there are very few of them today. In my survey, only 3.5% have this designation, or just 33 draught and 8 bottled beers. In terms of original gravity, they average only 1.041 (10.2 °P) and cover a range of 1.032–1.060 (8.0–14.7 °P), with one "flier" at 1.075

(18.2 °P). Clearly, the lower values are far away from historical levels; they can be discounted as just being brewers' attempts to cash in on tradition by calling low-strength bitter something it is not.

In the first edition of *Pale Ale*, I quoted a range of 1.050–1.055 (12.4–13.6 °P). This was based as much on an arbitrary division as on the few extant beers of this type, such as Worthington White Shield (which I am now inclined to class as a pale ale, rather than an IPA, as I said previously in the chapter). I now think that I was wrong here and that this range is far too narrow. The AHA quotes a much wider range, 1.050–1.070 (12.4–17.1 °P).[16] This is a better range for this substyle and just barely includes Hodgson's original version of IPA. However, the AHA does not include an American-style IPA in its listings, although these fall within the band for English-style IPAs. And there are a lot more examples of American IPAs that would fit this gravity band than there are of their English cousins!

American Substyles

Most recent books on American beers give only subjective taste comments and offer little in the way of technical information on the beers tasted. Few attempts have been made to draw all of this together into a single survey with detailed listings of original gravities, bittering levels, and so on. I am aware only of that by Steve Johnson.[17] In his book, *America's Best Brews*, he lists an amazing number of beers, all of which he has tasted himself. He also gives a fair bit of detail on individual beers. He does include ESB as a separate style, which I do not agree with, but his information is very useful.

An analysis of the pale ale category in Johnson's book is a good place to start when looking at the American versions of this beer. He lists 77 beers, which

FIGURE 3

Occurrence of American Pale Ales

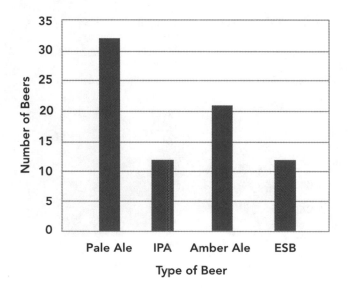

include 32 pale ales (41.6%), 12 IPAs (15.6%), 21 amber ales (27.3%), and 12 ESBs (15.6%). (There is, of course, no bitter category.) Figure 3 shows this breakdown graphically.

The figure indicates that American pale ale is far more common than any of the other three and that there are slightly more ambers than IPAs or ESBs. Of course, these are just numbers; they tell us nothing about volume consumption or about comparative strengths. It is therefore instructive to do the same as we did with bitters and look at the distribution of original gravities for each beer. This is shown in figure 4.

FIGURE 4

Distribution of Original Gravities for Bitter Ales

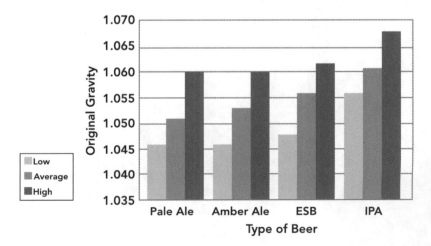

In each case, the middle bar is the average. As you can see, there is not a great deal of difference between pale and amber ales, while ESB is definitely higher. However, there is a lot of overlap, with the low of ESB being lower than the average for both pale and amber ales. IPA is definitely brewed to higher gravities than the other beers, but all average above 1.050, significantly higher than the average for many of the English beers.

Johnson also gives data on hop bitterness. However, it is more limited, covering only 47 of the total 77 rated. Figure 5 shows a plot of bitterness against beer style.

FIGURE 5

Hop Bitterness for American Pale Ales

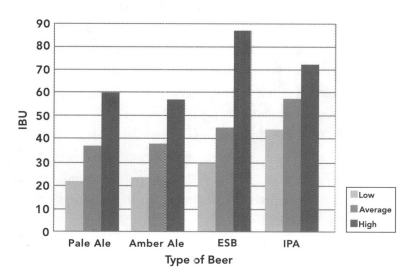

The figure shows some surprising results. Although bitterness levels are generally high (above 35 IBU on average), the amber ales are slightly more bitter than the pale ales! The IPAs, as you might expect, are clearly the most bitter beers, while those in the ESB category are significantly more bitter than the pale and amber ales (even allowing for the one very high result that somewhat skews the average). These results might be misleading, however, since they are based on a small sample that might not be fully representative.

What is significant about the ESB "style" is that Johnson defines it as beer produced in the style of a strong bitter. It does, in fact, fit exactly in the gravity range for English strong bitter. And that is where I propose to leave it, rather than designating it as a specific substyle. As I mentioned earlier, there is only one beer in England that is designated ESB (Fuller's ESB), and it does not particularly match this ESB "style," in my opinion. This is an arbitrary decision, I admit. These so-called ESB types are more bitter than their English counterparts and often are made from American ingredients, so they could be classed as a distinct subspecies, just as American pale ale and IPA are. But, English pale ales and IPAs are not as strongly represented as are their American cousins. Bitters are the dominant beers in England, and putting American ESB as a separate substyle is an unnecessary complication.

Having got that out of the way, next I discuss the separate American substyles.

American Pale Ales

From my analysis of Johnson's numbers (figure 5), American pale ales have an average gravity of 1.051 (12.6 °P). Thus, they pretty much fit in the middle of the gravity range I gave previously for the English types, 1.045–1.055 (11.2–13.6 °P). In each case, the AHA gives a slightly wider spread, 1.044–1.056 (11.0–13.8 °P).[18]

An interesting experiment was carried out in 1997 in which six Oregon brewers produced a pale ale from the same recipe. The purpose was to test differences obtained by different brewers using virtually identical ingredients.[19] The significance of that experiment for our purposes is that the brewers agreed that an original gravity of 1.058–1.060 (14.3–14.7 °P) was right for a Pacific Northwest pale ale. In my definition, this would be an American IPA! However, note that these "pale ales" were not all as bitter as some of the American IPAs quoted previously—they had IBU levels around 50, although a couple were closer to 60. But these IBUs do put them higher than the average of 37 IBUs shown in figure 5.

Apart from the ingredients, there is often one other important difference between English and American pale ales. The English versions have a definite fruity character due to esters produced by the strains of top-fermenting yeast used. American pale ales, particularly as typified by the classic Sierra Nevada version, do not. For the latter, a very clean fermenting yeast is used that gives little in the way of esters, so the beer is somewhat crisper in flavor than a typical English pale ale. It also is crisper than a typical strong bitter. The fruity nuances of a bitter are important. They give the beer complexity and prevent it from being one-dimensional because of the high hop bitterness, which can dominate all other flavors. American pale ales lose complexity from the presence of esters and rely on intense hop flavor instead, using hops at almost every stage in the brewing process. The result is a beer that is high in hop character, bitterness, and aroma.

American IPAs

American IPAs fit into the gravity range 1.050–1.070 (12.4–17.1 °P). Figure 4 shows a range of 1.056–1.068 (13.8–16.6 °P), with an average of 1.061 (15.0 °P). So the two sets of figures for English and American IPAs mesh nicely. But it is the raw materials that really distinguish these beers from their English relatives.

American pale and crystal malts are often used, but not exclusively, as some brewers still insist on using English pale malt. But the one, most important characteristic that distinguishes American IPAs is their uncompromising use of American hops. In particular, American craftbrewers use hops to give their IPAs a powerful and very distinctive aroma and character. Most notably, although by no means exclusively, Cascades hops are used for this purpose. The flowery, citruslike character of this hop is very different from anything that can be achieved using high-quality English hops such as Goldings and Fuggles.

But, perhaps even more important, the American IPAs are often quite high in hop bitterness. Bert Grant's "original" IPA is said to have had 60 IBU. In general, levels of 50–55 IBU are not rare, and Anderson Valley claims that its Hop Ottin IPA has as much as 90 IBU![20] In fact, as figure 5 shows, bitterness for American IPAs averages 58 IBU, with a range of 44–73! Note, however, that this survey of Johnson's numbers includes only seven samples as a basis. This is a fairly small sample population and might not be truly representative. Nevertheless, these are definitely bitter beers. In this, as in their original gravities, they can genuinely lay claim to being close to the original IPAs. And remember that there is ample evidence of Bass's having used American hops in the nineteenth century (but then, Cascades was not around at that time).

American Amber Ales

American amber ales are last on the list. Last perhaps because they are somewhat harder to classify, as brewers

Although it is located in sleepy rural Vermont, Catamount Brewing Company is one of America's most vibrant new breweries.

sometimes use this style name as a catchall term. Recall from chapter 1 that these beers were really American bitter in concept, but they lacked the name because it was regarded as a deterrent to the average consumer. Michael Jackson did not see fit to describe amber as a style in either of his two major books.[21] Indeed, he points out that the term *amber* is used almost as often to describe a lager. Even California Steam Beer, a trademark of Anchor Brewing Company, could be included in this category, in all respects but one. That is, it is a bottom-fermented beer and therefore a bastard style, like the cream ales I dismissed earlier.

Bitters cover a very wide range of color, so defining a substyle on the basis of color is something of a risky venture. Yet there are many "amber" beers that fit the pale

ale/bitter character in this country and that cannot be classified as either American pale ale or IPA.[22] They can be separated from English bitters, since many of them are bottled, although quite a few are draught beers. All, however, are more highly carbonated and served much colder than is the English norm. They are also largely produced from American ingredients, both malt and hops. However, it is not uncommon to use an English yeast, so such beers are often fruitier than American pale ales. Also, in most cases they are filtered and certainly not cask-conditioned.

Perhaps the most obvious defining characteristic of American amber ale should be its color. The AHA style guideline quotes 11–18 °SRM[23]—this puts such beers well within the normal range for bitter. Yet at least one amber is as high as 33 °SRM.[24] I would support this color level as also being appropriate to the amber style.

As for original gravity, figure 4 shows a range of 1.046–1.060 (11.4–14.7 °P), with an average of 1.053 (13.1 °P). The AHA guideline is 1.044–1.056 (11.0–13.8 °P). Thus, the two sets of figures agree fairly well, except at the top of the range. I have no argument against the AHA guideline, but it does specify a fairly narrow range. In fact, this makes a fairly interesting point. American micros tend not to brew low-gravity beers (just look at figure 4), while much of the output of English brewers is at original gravities below 1.040 (10.0 °P). This difference comes from cultural variations between American and English drinkers. The English pub, despite quite a few changes in recent years, is still a social center—a place for an evening's drinking, not eating. As a result, many drinkers, who still insist on drinking by the full English pint, do not want anything too strong. Rather, they want a "session" beer, one they can drink several pints of during the course of an evening, without falling over. In contrast, Amer-

FIGURE 6

The Pale Ale Family

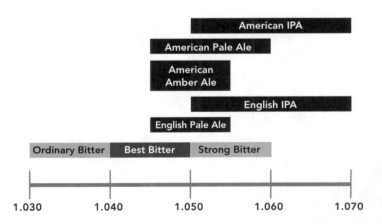

ican "pubs," and especially brewpubs, are primarily restaurants. The American pubgoer is interested in drinking a moderate amount of a beer that has a higher quality and strength. Although this is a sweeping generalization, there is a good deal of truth in it. However, I must point out that there are many English session bitters that do have a surprising amount of character and flavor.

Summary and Profiles of Pale Ales

Now we need to collate all of this information and to define these substyles in terms of original gravity, bitterness, color, post-fermentation treatment, method of dispense (bottle, keg, or cask), and temperature of serving. Figure 6 is an attempt to show the relation between the members of the pale ale style.

In tables 1, 2, and 3, I show the profiles for the members of the pale ale style.

For more information on beer styles, other than those sources already quoted, refer to *Designing Great Beers* by Ray Daniels and *The Essentials of Beer Style* by Fred Eckhardt listed in the notes—both are excellent books.[25] However, most of the information in the tables is from my own experience and knowledge—and sometimes it is pure opinion!

TABLE 1

Bitter Profiles

Specifications	Ordinary Bitter	Best Bitter	Strong Bitter
Original gravity	1.030–1.039	1.040–1.049	1.050–1.060
Original gravity (°P)	7.6–9.8	10.0–12.2	12.4–14.7
Final gravity	1.006–1.010	1.008–1.012	1.011–1.015
Final gravity (°P)	1.5–2.6	2.1–3.1	2.8–3.8
Apparent extract (%)	74–80	76–80	75–78
Alcohol by volume (%)	3.0–3.9	4.0–4.9	5.0–6.0
Alcohol by weight (%)	2.4–3.1	3.2–3.9	4.0–4.8
pH	3.9–4.2	3.9–4.2	3.9–4.2
Reducing sugars (%)	1.0–2.0	1.0–2.5	1.0–2.5
Acidity, as lactic acid (%)	0.05	0.05	0.05
Bitterness (IBU)	20–40	20–45	25–45
HBU (5 gallons)[1]	5–10	5–11	6–11
Color (°SRM)	5–15	5–20	5–25
Hop aroma/character	Moderate (dry hopping optional)	Moderate (dry hopping optional)	Moderate (dry hopping optional)
Esters[2]	Yes	Yes	Yes
Diacetyl (ppm)[3]	0.2 maximum	0.2 maximum	0.2 maximum
Pale malts	UK 2-rowed	UK 2-rowed	UK 2-rowed
Crystal malt[4]	Medium to dark	Medium to dark	Medium to dark
Hop source, bittering	English	English	English
Hop source, aroma	English/European	English/European	English/European
CO_2, volumes	1.0–1.5	1.0–1.5	1.0–1.5
Filtration	No	No	No
Dispense method[5]	Cask conditioned	Cask conditioned	Cask conditioned

[1]Calculated from IBU, this assumes 25% extraction of alpha acid.

[2]The dominant ester is ethyl acetate, but the mixture is complex. This should be noticeable in beer as pleasant fruitiness.

[3]Diacetyl flavor is acceptable but apparent only in some bitters.

[4]Normal range is 50–150 °SRM, depending on the brewer's taste; lighter crystal malts also sometimes used.

[5]Keg versions are usually filtered and pasteurized and served at up to 2.0 volumes CO_2; so-called smooth versions are served with mixed nitrogen/carbon dioxide.

TABLE 2

English Pale Ale and IPA Profiles

Specifications	English Pale Ale	English India Pale Ale
Original gravity	1.045–1.055	1.050–1.070
Original gravity (°P)	11.2–13.5	12.4–17.1
Final gravity[1]	1.010–1.014	1.012–1.016
Final gravity (°P)	2.6–3.6	3.1–4.1
Apparent extract (%)	75–78	76–77
Alcohol by volume (%)[2]	4.5–5.5	5.1–7.2
Alcohol by weight (%)[2]	3.6–4.4	4.1–5.7
pH	3.9–4.2	3.8–4.2
Reducing sugars (%)	1.0–2.0	1.0–2.5
Acidity, as lactic acid (%)[3]	0.05	0.05
Bitterness (IBU)	30–45	35–60
HBU (5 gallons)[4]	8–12	9–16
Color (°SRM)	8–14	8–14
Hop aroma/character	Moderate	Moderate (dry hopping optional)
Esters[5]	Yes	Yes
Diacetyl (ppm)[6]	0.2 maximum	0.2 maximum
Pale malts	UK 2-rowed	UK 2-rowed
Crystal malt[7]	Light to medium	Light to medium
Hop source, bittering	English	English/American[8]
Hop source, aroma	English	English
CO_2, volumes	1.5–2.5	1.0–2.0
Filtration[9]	Yes	Yes
Dispense method	Bottled; bottle conditioned	Cask or bottle conditioned; bottled

[1]Finishing gravity for IPAs might be lower if the ale is matured longer than is customary in England.
[2]Longer-matured beers will also be higher in alcohol than this range.
[3]If the ale is stored as original in wood for long periods, acidity is likely to be higher.
[4]Calculated from IBU, this assumes 25% extraction of alpha acid.
[5]Esters are for bitters but can be higher for IPAs.
[6]Diacetyl flavor is acceptable but not common.
[7]Normal range is 20–80 °SRM; these beers should be paler than bitters.
[8]American hops may be used, as Burton brewers did in the nineteenth century, but not Cascades!
[9]Filtration is usually used only for beers that are not naturally conditioned.

TABLE 3

American Amber, Pale Ales, and IPA Profiles

Specifications	Amber	Pale	IPA
Original gravity	1.044–1.056	1.045–1.055	1.050–1.070
Original gravity (°P)	11.0–13.8	11.2–13.6	12.4–17.1
Final gravity[1]	1.008–1.016	1.010–1.015	1.012–1.018
Final gravity (°P)	2.1–4.1	2.6–3.8	3.1–4.6
Apparent extract (%)	71–81	73–78	74–76
Alcohol by volume (%)	4.5–5.3	4.7–5.3	5.1–7.0
Alcohol by weight (%)	3.6–4.2	3.7–4.2	4.1–5.6
pH	3.9–4.2	3.9–4.2	3.9–4.2
Reducing sugars (%)	1.0–2.0	1.0–2.0	1.0–2.5
Acidity, as lactic acid (%)[2]	0.05	0.05	0.05
Bitterness (IBU)[3]	30–50	30–50	40–60
HBU (5 gallons)[4]	8–13	8–13	10–16
Color (°SRM)[5]	12–30	5–12	8–14
Hop aroma/character	Moderate	High	High
Esters[6]	Yes	No	Yes
Diacetyl (ppm)[7]	0.15 maximum	0.15 maximum	0.15 maximum
Pale malts	US 2-rowed/6-rowed	US 2-rowed	US 2-rowed
Crystal malt	Medium to dark[8]	Light to medium[9]	Light to medium[9]
Hop source, bittering	American	American	American/English
Hop source, aroma	American	American	American
CO_2, volumes	2.0–2.5	2.0–2.5	2.0–2.5
Filtration	Yes	Yes	Yes
Dispense method[10]	Bottled, draught	Bottled, draught, bottle conditioned	Bottled, draught, bottle conditioned

[1]Finishing gravity might be lower, depending on the length and method of maturation.

[2]Pale ale in particular should be low in acidity.

[3]My numbers for IBU differ from those of the AHA, which gives 20–40 for American pale ale. I think 20 is far too low for a beer that clearly should be bitter!

[4]Calculated from IBU, this assumes 25% extraction of alpha acid.

[5]This is a wider range for amber than that given by AHA to include current commercial samples. Pale ale is normally the palest of all these beers.

[6]Esters should be very low for pale ale, with little perceived, although traces are acceptable.

[7]Diacetyl should not normally be perceived, although traces are acceptable.

[8]Amber needs dark crystal malts, in the range of 80–150 °SRM.

[9]Pale ale and IPA should use malts in the range of 20–60 °SRM.

[10]This can be cask conditioned or served unfiltered from a cellar tank.

Some important aspects are not included in the tables. One is the yeast used. All of these beers are produced by top-fermenting ale yeasts, fermenting at "warm" temperatures (60–70 °F, 15–21 °C); I discuss the use of yeasts in pale ale in more depth in chapter 3.

Another is the serving temperature. The traditional and desirable range is the typical "cellar" temperature in England, 52–55 °F (11–13 °C). However, there has been a tendency to decrease these temperatures somewhat, even in England, through techniques such as the use of in-line coolers. And in America, beer drinkers do tend to drink beer significantly colder than this. I know all of the arguments about America's having a warmer climate than England's, and there is some validity in them. In the U.S. Northeast during summer, beer at close to ambient temperatures would be quite undrinkable. But, then why do we drink it at these same cold temperatures in the winter when the temperature is below freezing?

Beers of this type at temperatures much below 50 °F (10 °C) lose a great deal of their flavor and complexity. If this is coupled with high carbon dioxide levels, the result is quite bland. This is because these two conditions kill off the fruity character and the hop aroma and character. They even kill off the hop bitterness on the palate, and above all, these are beers that should taste bitter! Any

An old coaching inn, the White Hart in Overton, Hampshire, still functions as an inn, although the main roads no longer pass through the village and the beer is not as good as it used to be.

brewer—big, small, professional, or amateur—who attempts to dumb down this aspect of pale ale character has totally missed the point, and we would all be better off if the brewer turned to some other occupation!

CHAPTER 3

Brewing
Pale Ales

There are no secrets to brewing quality pale ales. The techniques used in brewing this beer are basic, and they are not dealt with directly in this chapter. Rather, I take the approach that the selection of ingredients—malt, hops, yeast, and water—is the most important decision that the pale ale brewer makes. Therefore, I discuss these ingredients in the light of both traditional and modern practices of pale ale production, as well as offer some ideas for experimentation.

It is not possible here to go into great detail, but where necessary some comments on the chemistry of the brewing process are addressed. Chapter 3 discusses the range of malts and their suitability in pale ale brewing. It also includes a look at available hop varieties, as well as the different forms of hop products available, and indicates how they should be used. Yeast selection, along with fermentation conditions and equipment, is also covered. Finally, I deal with the question of water treatment, discussing its importance to the brewing of quality pale ales and attempting to give a simple approach to the adjustment of mineral content of brewing water.

Brewing Techniques

The traditional basic brewing procedure for pale ales was very simple and was in place before pale ale emerged as a style. It started with two-rowed pale malt, mashed by a single-temperature infusion process. The collected wort was boiled with the bittering hops, perhaps with aroma hops added towards the end of the boil. Top-fermenting yeast was used in open fermenters, at "warm" temperatures. The green beer then was racked into wooden casks, along with an additional few extra hops and perhaps finings. After several months of cool conditioning, the beer was ready to drink.

Two or three hundred years ago, this process could be very much hit or miss. Mash temperatures were very approximate, determined by whether the brewer could see his reflection in the hot liquor before striking the grain. Wort cooling was carried out by holding the hopped wort in long, shallow, wooden vessels, which were often situated in the roof area of the brew house, exposing the beer to bird droppings and insects as well as bacteria. Fermentation temperatures were not controlled and depended on ambient conditions—this is why brewing was normally not carried out in the summer. Other aspects of the process, such as yeast handling, were also very careless by modern standards.

For many modern English brewers, these procedures have hardly changed, although the introduction of instrumentation and a vastly improved understanding of the whole brewing process has led to much better control of each stage. Other brewers have incorporated nontraditional techniques, such as whirlpool separation of the trub, closed fermentation vessels, filtration, cold storage, pasteurization, forced carbonation, and carbon dioxide or even mixed-gas dispense. I am assuming that you already have a knowledge of basic brewing techniques, so I do not go through any of these in detail here (except for dispensing techniques,

FIGURE 7

Brewing Unit Processes

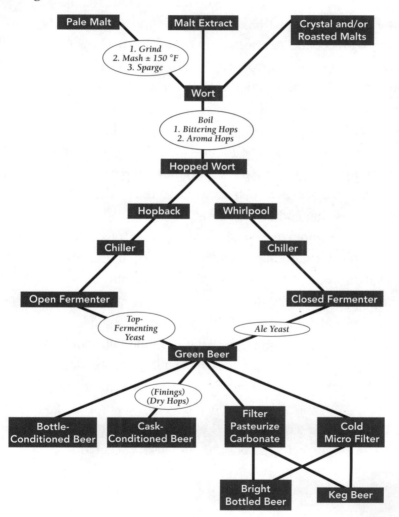

which are discussed in the next chapter). However, when I discuss ingredients I do make some comments about these processes as they apply to pale ale brewing. As a guide, figure 7 is a schematic flowchart of the various processes.

As complicated as this chart may seem, it does not include several steps that might be taken by modern brewers. For example, not shown is that cask- and bottle-conditioned beers are often primed with sugar at racking. Sugar, an adjunct popular with many English brewers, is added directly to the wort kettle. Also not shown is that cask- and bottle-conditioned beers can be *kraeusened* (primed with a portion of fermenting wort), although this is not a common practice.

Further, when producing bottle-conditioned beers, many brewers filter the green beer and then redose it with yeast at bottling. This gives them good control over the yeast count in the bottle and permits the use of a different yeast than that used in the fermentation. The brewer might, for example, want a strain with good sedimentation characteristics in the bottle and a powdery, nonflocculent strain in the fermenter in order to achieve good attenuation.

Also not pictured in the chart are techniques of pasteurization. These are beyond the scope of this book and not appropriate to the homebrewer. However, craftbrewers with far-reaching distribution lines might sometimes consider it necessary. Personally, I do not recommend it because it can easily spoil the flavor of the beer, regardless of what it might do for stability. A better technique for the craftbrewer worried about beer degradation in distribution is sterile membrane filtration. Filtration is commonly practiced in commercial bright beer production but is a technique also available to the homebrewer.[1] Note that filtration of any kind will likely have a deleterious effect on big, highly hopped beers because it removes both some hop flavor and some bitterness and adversely affects foam formation. Despite the difficulties involved, these beers are undoubtedly at their best when served in the draught, cask-conditioned form.

Malt

Malt is the main source of fermentables in a beer. The bulk of these fermentables, whether you are using extract or grain, comes from pale malt. This base malt also provides other important elements such as foam-forming protein products, dextrins that help give the beer body, and nitrogenous and mineral compounds that yeast needs to give a healthy fermentation. More highly roasted malts, such as crystal and caramel malts, add color, flavor, and body to the finished beer.

In this section, I discuss the various malts and their suitability in pale ale brewing. This includes not only those malts that traditionally have been used to produce pale ale, but also deals with the possibility of using non-traditional malts, such as Munich and brown malt. I also make some comments as to how malts should be used, dealing with malt extract separately and with mashing techniques for pale malts, as well as with when and where to add roasted malts.

Malt Extracts

The dominant flavor aspects of pale ales are hop character and flavor, so pale ales are well suited to brewing with malt extracts. You can obtain a variety of extract-based kits to cover the whole range of these beers—from ordinary bitter to IPA. This is the simplest approach to brewing. Unfortunately, it often leaves a lot to be desired. Some of these kits are not as informative as they might be. For example, one of the more comprehensive kit guides does not mention any requirement for the addition of sugar![2] And then, too, many kits recommend that ridiculously large amounts of sugar be used. They also might offer brewing instructions that if followed will not give a quality beer, to say the least. Further, the literature is not much help because it includes little guidance on kits, although the various brewing magazines do occasionally review individual kits.

What is worse for the pale ale style is that kit beers are almost invariably underhopped, lacking in both bitterness and hop character. Perhaps the biggest disadvantage of kits and hopped extracts, though, is that manufacturers do not offer information on bittering levels. Thus, you have no idea what you are going to get until you have actually brewed the beer.

Not all kits are bad. The better ones offer an excellent introduction to the art and craft of brewing. But such kits do almost everything for you, leaving no room for creativity on your part. I have no doubt that you will find that a much more interesting and enjoyable result can be obtained with plain, unhopped extracts, with you adding your own bittering and aroma hops. The best results, I believe, will be obtained with those kits and recipes that do not require added sugar, but which use only malt. I strongly believe that any kit or recipe that requires the use of sugar will give better results if you use the same weight of dry malt extract in place of the sugar.

Types of malt extracts. All malt extracts are not equal, as some manufacturers include significant amounts of corn or invert sugar syrup along with the malt. Malt extracts often suffer from low levels of free amino nitrogen (FAN) in the wort—this is a common cause of stuck or incomplete fermentation.[3] Using sugar in place of malt only exacerbates this problem and can lead to the production of some strange flavors. I deal with this issue later in this chapter in the section under sugars. The point is that you should be careful in your choice of extract and be prepared to experiment until you find which brands suit your taste.

You should go with extracts designed for pale ale, bitter, or amber ale brewing. I think it is best to use plain extracts—this will give you the greatest amount of room to express your own creativity. In any case, the hopped versions are often inadequately hopped for this style, so you will have to add hops anyway. Although there is little public information available on manufacturing methods, most manufacturers seem to use a combination of hop extracts and hop oils rather than pellet or flower hops.[4] However, in general, I find that hopping with extracts and oils does not give the clean bitterness and spicy, flowery, aromatic flavors and aromas that can be achieved with pellets and flowers. (See the section on hops later in this chapter.)

I cannot recommend individual extracts, since there are so many of them. Essentially all are produced by a similar process of evaporation. What is being concentrated is a brewing wort. The exact composition of that wort can, like any wort, vary greatly according to the ingredients and formulation used. Thus, the extracts produced come in a wide variety and are usually regarded as proprietary products by the producers. For further useful advice on malt extract selection, refer to the suggested reading list in appendix B.

Using malt extract. Liquid extracts should give a gravity yield of around 1.036 (9.0 °P) for 1 pound made to 1 gallon with water, while dry extracts should yield about 1.045 (11.2 °P) under the same conditions. Nitrogen levels for liquid extracts should be about 0.07% or more, while dry extracts should give at least 0.1% nitrogen. Extracts quoting high-gravity yields coupled with low nitrogen are a sure sign of dilution with sugar of some sort. They should be avoided.

Although hoppiness in all of its aspects is the primary flavor component of such beers, you still want some malt character as well so that the beer's flavor is not completely one-dimensional. Even with high-quality extracts, you will find it necessary to add extra body and flavor by including crystal and/or roasted malts (see later sections on this in this chapter).

It might also be advantageous to use the *partial mash approach*. This approach involves adding a pound or two of pale malt, mashing it at ±150 °F (65.6 °C), collecting the wort, adding the extract, and then boiling in the usual way. Partial mashing not only adds a little extra flavor, it also helps to ensure adequate levels of FAN in the wort.

Another point about extract brewing is that it is common practice for the boil volume to be much smaller than the final brew volume. Typically, for 5 gallons of finished beer, only 2–3 gallons are used in the boil. This means that the specific gravity of the wort boiled is much higher than that of the wort at fermentation. There is nothing wrong in doing this. However, extraction of the bittering principles of the hops is less efficient at high gravities than at low gravities. In other words, for the same bittering levels you will need more hops for such a concentrated boil than you would need using all-grain mashing procedures. I deal with that in the hops section later in this chapter.

Over-boiling of malt extract can also be a problem, depending on the method of manufacture. If it has been taken to a full-length boil and the formation of hot break, before being concentrated, further boiling might result in low protein/peptide levels in the wort. The result is a thin beer that lacks both body and head retention. It is best to keep the boil to around 45 minutes, up to 60 minutes at a maximum, to avoid this, rather than boil for the more normal 90 minutes used for a full-mash wort. One manufacturer recommends as little as 20 minutes of boiling for a pale beer.[5] These relatively short boil times result in decreased rates of hop usage, so the amount of hops used have to be increased to achieve the desired level of bitterness. Putting the two factors of a short and a concentrated boil together, you might have to use as much as 50 to 100% more bittering hops than would be needed for a similar original gravity beer brewed only from grain malt.

Color is often a problem with liquid malt extracts. When liquid malt extract is stored for a long time, darkening reactions can occur. This can make it very difficult to achieve the right hue for the paler types of pale ales, such as the "golden bitters." It might also cause the production of unwanted oxidized flavors. So you should try to buy from a supplier that has a good turnover of stock.

Dry extracts are a better bet because they do not undergo such reactions. If you want a darker color, you can best achieve this by adding crystal or roasted malts, which will also enhance the flavor through the introduction of nutty, caramel nuances.

Do not be discouraged from using malt extracts in the brewing of pale ales. A good many extract beers of this style have won prizes in competitions.[6] True, you will find it easier to obtain a balanced wort and reproducible fermentations when working with all-grain malt recipes than with extract-based formulations. But the main flavor aspects of pale ales come from the hops and from the fruity flavors delivered by the yeast. With good-quality extract, careful use of hops, and a choice yeast, there is no reason why you cannot brew an excellent pale ale, based on extract alone.

There is a strong argument that you will always get better results from all-grain brewing than you will from extract brewing. But using grain malt does not guarantee success. It is impossible to brew good beer from bad-quality ingredients, no matter how good your techniques are. But using quality ingredients might not be enough, either, if your techniques are poor. Any expert brewer worth his salt should be able to make a good pale ale or bitter from extract.

Pale Malt

Pale malt is the foundation stone for pale ale brewing, whether you are mashing or using an extract. For the paler, golden brews, it might be the only source of color and fermentables. So you should use pale malt of the highest quality, that designed for brewing just this type of beer. In the first edition of *Pale Ale*, I stated that this highest-quality malt was British malt, which I referred to only in generic terms. Now, all that has changed. Today, a variety of pale malts are available to both the home-brewer and craftbrewer.

Types of pale malt. There are two basic divisions of pale malt, named after the nature of the barley from which they are produced:

- six-rowed pale malt
- two-rowed pale malt

Six-rowed pale malt is the major malt for the brewing of American factory beers. This is primarily because it is high both in nitrogen and in enzymes, thereby making it ideal for brewing beers that have a high level of adjuncts, as is typical of American mainstream pale lagers. It can be used in pale ale brewing and can even give a halfway decent beer (provided hops and yeast are carefully chosen). Six-rowed pale malt also gives slightly lower extract yield than two-rowed malt. Further, it can give chill haze problems unless extra processing steps are taken, such as enzyme addition, silica-gel treatment, or polyvinylpyrrolidone treatment. Most brewers also consider that six-rowed malt gives a beer of inferior flavor compared to one produced from two-rowed malt. Unless you want to make a high-adjunct beer, you should work only with two-rowed pale malt. Since I strongly recommend that you work on a malt-only basis if you wish to brew top-quality pale ales (see the adjuncts section later in this chapter), two-rowed pale malt is the only way to go.

Six-rowed pale malts are designed for high-adjunct lager production. Thus, they are fairly lightly malted and kilned so as to keep a high level of enzymes and a very low color (1–2 °SRM). Such malts are also high in nitrogen (11–12% as total protein). They are sometimes referred to as *undermodified*, which means that the malting process has not gone as far to completion as is usually the case with ale malts. A consequence of this is that such malts require multistep mashing, with rests at two or more different temperatures. In particular, they need a protein rest in order to reduce in the beer the levels of high molecular weight protein degradation products, which are major causes of chill haze problems. This protein rest is usually at 120–130 °F (49–54 °C). It may be followed by rests at various temperatures before the final saccharification rest at ±150 °F (65.6 °C).

In general, two-rowed pale malts are more completely germinated during malting and are kilned at slightly higher temperatures than six-rowed malts. Two-rowed malts usually are higher in color (2–3 °SRM), lower in nitrogen (9–10% as total protein), and lower in enzymes. They are often called highly modified malts, meaning that a protein degradation step is not necessary in mashing. A one-temperature saccharification rest is all that is required to convert starch to fermentable sugars. Although low in enzyme content, modern two-rowed pale malts are actually high enough in enzyme content to convert up to about 20% starch adjuncts, as well as their own starch content. Properly handled, they will give 1–2% more extract than six-rowed malts, although this small difference will rarely be important to either homebrewers or craftbrewers, either in terms of cost or efficiency.

More important, two-rowed malts give good results with the classic single-temperature infusion mash at ±150 °F (65.6 °C). I say plus or minus (±) because the exact temperature depends very much on what you want to achieve. You might wish to go a degree or two lower to ensure good fermentability and high attenuation, a feature of the early Burton IPAs. Or, you might wish to go as much as five degrees higher in order to give the beer more body. This could be particularly desirable in, say, a golden or

American pale ale with no added crystal malt. The variety of pale ales now on the market in Britain and America encompasses a range of fermentabilities and permits you to choose the same.

It can be argued that a single-temperature infusion mash is not optimum for two-rowed pale malts. A 30-minute rest at 104 °F (40 °C) before proceeding to saccharification temperatures has been recommended as improving mash yields by as much as 15%.[7] I have used such a rest myself for some years because I found that it did improve my own extract yield. Of course, for the homebrewer this might not be important in the same financial sense that it is to a major factory brewer. However, I have found that this approach not only improves the yield, but also makes it much more reproducible. This makes it possible to hit target gravities just about every time—even with entirely new recipes—which makes the whole job of recipe formulation much simpler.

In *An Analysis of Brewing Techniques*, George and Laurie Fix recommend running a three-step mash at 104/140/158 °F (40/60/70 °C).[8] My standard approach is just two steps for beers in the pale ale style: 104/155 °F (40/68 °C). Note that for these highly modified two-rowed malts, a protein rest at 115–130 °F (46–54 °C) should be avoided, as it will adversely affect both foam and malt flavor.

The single-temperature approach has the great benefits of being easy to operate and requiring relatively simple equipment. The homebrewer armed only with a spoon and a pot on a stove will find it a lot easier to run at only one temperature, than to go through several rests, for what might be only a small advantage in yield and flavor. And the craftbrewer might have no choice. Cost considerations often dictate that a mash tun be installed with no heating facility, and of course a lauter tun will not be needed with this technique. Many American craftbrewers as well as English traditional brewers have stayed with single-temperature infusion and still produce some very good bitters and pale ales. A further point is that these highly modified malts are easier to grind and crush. They also are much less likely to cause the dreaded "stuck mash," where wort cannot filter through the grain bed.

In the first version of *Pale Ale*, I simply recommended the use of British pale malt, but to do the same here would trivialize the current situation, both for homebrewers and craftbrewers. Now we have a whole variety of pale malts available from both England and America. These include, in addition to the more standard pneumatic malts, blended malts from several barleys and malts from single barleys, such as Maris Otter, Halcyon, and Klages. Also included are American malts specifically designed for pale

ale brewing and even traditional English floor-malted products. It is impossible here to consider each in detail, so table 4 features some representational analyses for the various products offered.

Malt Analysis

It would pay the craftbrewer (and probably the home-brewer!) to carefully read the malt analysis of every batch received. This is especially true if you are changing malts or if you want to create special effects. In the recent past, maltsters generally produced their products to the specifications of the bigger brewers, but that is no longer the case. Many of them now make malts targeted to the craftbrewer (and therefore suitable for the homebrewer). You

TABLE 4

Typical Analyses of Pale Malts

Specifications	British 2-rowed	U.S. 2-rowed	U.S. 6-rowed
Moisture (%)	1.5–3.0	2.0–4.0	3.0–4.0
Nitrogen, as total protein (%)	8.5–10.0	10.5–12.0	12.0–13.0
Total nitrogen (%)	1.4–1.7	1.7–1.9	1.9–2.1
Total soluble nitrogen (%)	0.5–0.7	0.6–0.9	0.9–1.1
Diastatic Power (°Lintner)	40–70	100–130	130–150+
Color (°SRM)	2.0–3.5	1.5–4.0	1.0–2.0
Extract (%)	80–82	79–81	77–80
Extract (as gravity/lb./U.S. gallon)	36–38	35–37	32–35

should select your malt on the basis of what you want to do and on the limitations of your equipment. A good look at malt specifications and analyses can save you a lot of effort and time and help you avoid costly errors. Of course, reading these is not always easy because the units of measurement are not completely standardized. For example, English malts might quote analyses according to EBU rather than the American Society of Brewing Chemists (ASBC) standards. Brewer and author Greg Noonan has written two helpful articles on this (see appendix B).

For comparisons among various malts and detailed background on malt analyses, homebrewers should read the articles listed in appendix B, which also includes a source on analytical methods.

The extract figures in table 4 are based on the extract laboratory test ASBC Methods of Analysis Malt-4.[9] They represent the maximum possible yields obtained by a much more efficient mash procedure than is possible in a real brewing context. You will therefore get lower yields in your brewery, depending on the efficiency of your grinding, mashing, and wort separation techniques. The craftbrewer might get fairly close to these numbers. However, he will have to determine the actual number by experiment. This should take only a few brews, provided good records are kept.

The homebrewer, too, should determine what sort of yield is obtainable, but much lower values are likely. A yield of 1.030 (7.6 °P)/pound/U.S. gallon is fairly good for any pale malt (and higher than quoted in many published recipes!). Note that the terminology I use here means the specific gravity of 1 U.S. gallon of wort obtained by mashing 1 pound of malt. It is easily obtained by dividing the gravity of a wort by the weight of malt used in pounds and the volume in U.S. gallons. I find it a simple way to measure performance, and one that readily adapts to the formulation of different beers.

Perhaps the most important point is to aim for consistency of yield; otherwise, you will have difficulty in hitting target gravities. If you are constantly striving to improve your techniques, it is possible to do much better than this. I routinely obtain 1.033–1.034 (8.3–8.5 °P)/pound/U.S. gallon in my set-up.

One final factor can easily throw off extract determinations: the moisture content of the malt. This should not be a problem for craftbrewers, who use up their shipments fairly quickly, but it might be for homebrewers who buy in bulk. Try to store the malt in a cool, dry place, preferably in a sealed container—this will also reduce the risk of insect contamination. If you use preground malt, buy only as much as you are going to use in a week or so, as this malt very readily picks up moisture from the atmosphere and spoils quickly.

Notice that I make no recommendation as to which is the best pale malt. There are a limited number of maltsters in Britain and America, and they all produce high-quality malt. Regardless of which you choose, you are unlikely to get anything that is poorly modified and difficult to handle. And for American pale ales, IPAs, and amber ales, you are committed to American malts, if you want to stay true to style. The converse that bitters and English pale ales should be made from British malts also holds true but is less definitive.

Malts produced by the older floor-malting process generally give better flavors than those made by modern pneumatic methods in drum maltings. The former is more expensive and now produced only on a limited scale, but many traditional English brewers still will use nothing else for this style of beer. Floor-malted Maris Otter is usually held to be the best and is now available even to the homebrewer. I find that it gives excellent results, especially in those beers with little added crystal malt. For some unknown reason, I get slightly lower yields with this than with more standard English pale malts. It tends to be a plump grain, which probably does not grind quite so well in my own set-up, but it should give the craftbrewer no problems in this respect. I recommend that you try this malt yourself.

Caramel and Crystal Malts

Caramel and crystal malts are widely used in pale ale brewing, especially for American amber ales and English bitters. They are very useful for lower-gravity beers because they add some color, mainly a reddish hue, as well as a nutty, caramel flavor and body, or mouthfeel.

Caramel malt. Caramel malt is produced from fully modified green malt that is taken before kilning so that it still contains a considerable amount of moisture. It is then stewed at temperatures of up to 160 °F (71 °C) in a closed vessel so that virtually no moisture escapes. Under these conditions, which are like those of mashing, the malt starch is broken down into sugars. A certain amount of caramelization and coloring occurs (through Maillard browning reactions) as this mixture is further heated, up to as high as 240 °F (116 °C) for the darker grades.

Many years ago, when I started brewing, it was possible to obtain only one grade of caramel malt, very dark in color. Now it is possible, even for the amateur, to obtain a whole range of such malts, varying in color 10–150 °SRM and with a corresponding increasing intensity of flavor.

While many of these do come from Britain, there is also a wide range manufactured in America. The latter include the so-called carastan or dextrin malts, which are very low in color (2–3 °SRM) and designed to give a beer body and mouthfeel, with little effect on color. The latter are really meant for lager brewing and are probably not appropriate for bitters and amber ales, in which the brewer is looking for the extra flavor provided by a crystal malt. However, they might be worth looking at for very pale or golden pale ale types.

Also in this category and available even to homebrewers are the Belgian CaraVienne, CaraMunich, and Special B malts. These range from 15 to 250 °SRM and have a distinctive biscuity flavor. Again, they are not really intended for use in pale ale brewing. In fact, many brewers might regard them as not suitable, certainly not for a pale ale or IPA. I have tried them in small amounts (2–3 % of the grist only) in some of my lower-gravity bitter ales and have found that they did add an extra dimension of complexity to what can otherwise be a rather thin beer.

Crystal malts. Crystal malts are used at rates of up to 10% of the total grist (or about 0.5 pound in 5 U.S. gallons) for a 1.048 (12 °P) pale ale. However, 5% is probably the maximum amount of the darkest grades.

Otherwise, the beer's flavor will be too coarse for this style. Crystal malts are generally added to the mash in all-grain brewing, although they contain no enzymes. All of the sugars and flavors are fully water-soluble and can be extracted by a simple steeping procedure, so these malts are quite suitable for extract brewing. In general, these yield slightly lower amounts of extract than pale malts. They also can be somewhat variable in their yield. However, since only a small amount is used, this variation should have little effect on the final gravity of the beer.

An important contribution of crystal malt to pale ale is color. Crystal malt adds a reddish hue, depending upon the degree of roasting and on the amount added to the mash. However, if you are looking at crystal malt solely for its color effect, and desire reproducible results, choosing the type and amount of crystal malt is not a simple matter. Beer color depends on a number of factors other than that contributed directly by the malt bill. The only real way to determine the color is by measurement, for which there are relatively simple methods available, as described by Ray Daniels in *Designing Great Beers*.[10] However, you can make approximate calculations as to the color to be expected from a given malt bill. Simply multiply the weight of each malt by its color rating, add the products, and divide by the volume in gallons. While only

TABLE 5

Typical Analyses for Crystal Malts

Specifications	Pale	Medium	Dark
Moisture (%)	3.0–7.0	3.5–6.0	3.0–6.0
Color (°SRM)	10–40	40–80	80–150
Extract (%)	60–65	60–65	60–65
Extrac, as gravity/ lb./U.S. gallon	25–30	25–30	25–30
Suitable for*	Pale, golden ales	IPA, bitters	Bitters, amber ales

*These are just guidelines, not limitations!

an approximation, this easy calculation does enable you to predict how different recipes with very similar processing steps might compare.

Be aware, however, that there are often significant batch-to-batch differences in the color of crystal malts. A variation of 10 °SRM for the lighter-colored grades is common, while the very dark grades might vary by as much as 30 °SRM. Most of these malts are proprietary products and might even give different flavors for the same color rating, depending on the manufacturer. You will have to experiment to find what suits your taste. There is less information about these in the literature than there is on pale ales, although there is still more than there used to be.[11] Table 5 summarizes typical crystal malt analyses.

If the range of commercial crystal malts does not suit you, you can make your own. The suggested reading list in appendix B offers several methods for doing this. These start basically with pale malt (usually after it has been soaked in water) that is heated first at 150 °F (66 °C) for one hour or so and then at 350 °F (177 °C) for up to two hours. The exact regime depends on the color desired; however, color determination will probably be difficult because the sample is unlikely to be uniform. I cannot tell you how well this works, as I have not tried it myself. The result likely will differ some from the commercial varieties because the extract starts from pale malt (which has been dried) and not from green malt. One advantage of this, however, is that the "crystal" malt would be fresh. Generally, using fresh malt makes a beer having better flavor with all roasted malts.

Other Malts

There is some, although fairly limited, leeway for using malts other than pale and crystal in this type of beer. Many English brewers do use them, however, although you must remember that they are making relatively low-gravity beers, where some tinkering with the grain bill can add to the beer's malt character. Other malts available include wheat, Munich, roasted, and brown.

Wheat malt. Foremost among these other available malts is wheat malt. This malt is added primarily for its head retention characteristics. Added at the rate of around 5% of the total grain bill, it helps in head retention for a beer at an original gravity of under 1.040 (10.0 °P). A beer with this original gravity is served at low carbonation levels, especially if other adjuncts are used.

Wheat malt at 1.5–3.0 °SRM has a similar effect on color as pale malt. It gives a slightly higher yield—82–85%, 1.036–1.039 (9.0–9.8 °P)/pound/U.S. gallon. It further has sufficient enzymes for full starch conversion that, when the malt is used in this sort of proportion, will not hinder wort run-off. I formerly used it in all of my pale ales. I have since concluded that it is not really necessary, with all-malt beers brewed at gravities above 1.045 (11.2 °P). The malt extract brewer might well consider it, but only if he uses the partial mash technique. This is because it must be mashed and cannot be added in a steep with crystal malt.

Munich malt. An interesting American variation is the inclusion of Munich malt by some pale ale brewers. This malt is kilned at slightly higher temperatures than pale malt, so it has a higher color (3–20 °SRM). It still gives a good extract yield at 77–81%, 1.032–1.037 (8.0–9.3 °P)/

pound/U.S. gallon and has sufficient enzymes to ensure good starch conversion. So it could be used at 10–20% of the grist if desired.

The higher-colored grades darken the beer just a shade, but its main effect—albeit a somewhat negative one—is in the area of flavor. It should add a little body and mouthfeel to the beer, but little in the way of the caramel flavors associated with crystal malts. The name tells you that it is not really intended for pale ale brewing. But there is no reason why you should not try it if you think it appropriate (although my preference is crystal malt).

Roasted malt. A number of British brewers go to the other extreme and use roasted malts such as chocolate or black malt. These should be used in very small amounts, say 1–2% of the grist, or about 1 ounce in a 5-gallon brew. I recommend doing this only for lower-gravity beers, where just a hint of roast character adds a little extra complexity to the beer.

Brown malt. Another possible variation is brown malt. As far as I know, no commercial brewer has tried it. This is a British product, relatively new to the American market and one really meant for use in porters above all. It is made from pale malt and has a caramel, biscuity flavor somewhere between crystal and Belgian malts. Its color is moderately high at around 50 °SRM, and the extract is fairly low at around 65%, or about 1.030 (7.6 °P)/pound/U.S. gallon. I have used it in a bitter at around 4% of the grist (5 ounces in a 5-gallon brew length) at 1.042 (10.5 °P). The result was a beer quite different from the usual bitter, with a distinctive caramel, nutty flavor. I recommend you try it. But do not overdo it because the flavor is strong enough to mask much of the hop character.

Adjuncts

Adjuncts essentially are sugars and cereals, such as corn or rice, that add fermentables but not flavor. American craftbrewers and many English microbrewers do not use them. However, the major English companies, as well as some of the regionals, persist in incorporating them into their beers. The usual story is that the adjuncts are nitrogen diluents, that is, they reduce the total amount of proteinaceous materials in the beer for a given original gravity. This then reduces the risk of chill haze formation in the finished product.

I do not buy this argument. If the beer is to be served at around 50–55 °F (10–13 °C), which a traditional pale

ale should be, then chill haze should not be a problem. If it is to be served colder, then the beer likely will be chilled and filtered anyway, thereby limiting the effects of chill haze. Besides, adjuncts are used only at the rate of 15–20% in normal English practice. I cannot believe that this rate can make or break the formation of haze.

Adjuncts might originally have been used in Britain simply because they were cheaper than malt. Using them for that reason might no longer be the case. It appears that cane sugar is more expensive (in terms of cost for extract obtained) than pale malt and that brewing syrups might be similar in cost per unit extract to pale malt.[12] This means that their only real benefits in brewing are in helping to control fermentability and in acting as brew extenders. These assets are of little use to the home-brewer, unless brewing something like a strong barley wine. Nor does this make them of much use to the craft-brewer, who is looking for a beer of character and does not want to risk losing quality for the sake of shaving a few pennies off costs.

Although a variety of cereal grains are used by the "factory" brewers of the world, their use in pale ale brewing is relatively limited. One good reason for this is that two-rowed pale malt cannot handle a lot of added starch because of its relatively low enzyme content. The types of adjunct used also are limited by the fact that most brewers use single-temperature infusion. Adjuncts that need cooking, such as rice, simply complicate temperature control. Further, the extra expense of a cereal cooker means that they offer little savings.

British brewers have used a variety of starch adjuncts from time to time. This happened notably during World War II, when a general shortage of raw materials led some to experiment even with potatoes as a source of starch. However, as noted previously, most brewers generally prefer the use of sugars or syrups.

None of these additives, as I think they are more accurately called, do anything for beer flavor. The high hop rates of pale ales require that malt contribute flavor in order to avoid the beer's becoming completely one-sided. Thus, I am convinced that using all-malt grists is the only acceptable way to brew quality pale ales. My mind is not completely closed, however. There are some beers that I know were brewed with adjuncts, and I have enjoyed them greatly. But I ask whether they would have been better still if they had been brewed from malt only.

Nevertheless, I briefly discuss the most common adjuncts, should you want to try them: sugar, corn syrup or barley-based syrup, and corn (flaked maize).

Sugar

Sugar comes in various forms, as described by Jeff Frane in his *Zymurgy* article, "How Sweet It Is: Brewing with Sugar."[13] Traditionally, British brewers used either cane sugar, which is a disaccharide and virtually 100% sucrose, or invert sugar, which is a 1:1 mixture of the monosaccharides fructose and dextrose. Invert generally is produced from various forms of sucrose. In America, the use of sugars of this type has been relatively rare, although corn sugar, which is also virtually 100% dextrose, has been used extensively in homebrewing.

Sucrose is not directly fermentable by yeast. Rather, it is rapidly hydrolyzed to fermentable monosaccharides by yeast enzymes. This happens especially when it is used at the rate of only 10–15% of the grist. At this level, it will not yield a cidery flavor. This happens only when so much sugar is used that there is insufficient FAN to act as a yeast nutrient. Sucrose gives an extract of 1.046 (11.4 °P)/pound/U.S. gallon, while invert and corn sugar will give around 1.036 (9 0 °P)/pound/U.S. gallon, because both contain around 20% moisture. All of this extract is fully fermentable by yeast. This permits you to go to high attenuation of the beer, which is one way to achieve the low finishing gravities obtained in some of the early IPAs.

Note that there is nothing wrong with using sugar for priming, where you are looking for something readily fermentable that will not alter beer flavor.

Corn Syrup and Barley-Based Syrup

There has been a general move by commercial brewers toward the use of corn syrup (maize) or even barley-based syrup. These are produced by chemical or enzymatic hydrolysis of the grain starches. They may even be produced in forms that contain no mineral salts. More important, they can be made to match almost any carbohydrate spectrum, with almost any degree of fermentability. Barley syrups can even be made to be nearly identical to an all-malt wort. For more information on these syrups, see appendix B.

Corn (Flaked Maize)

Probably the only such adjunct worthy of any note is corn. Corn is used most commonly in pale ales in the form of flaked maize. Flaked maize is manufactured by milling the corn, a process that removes the grain hull and germ, leaving only the endosperm in the form of grits. Grits are used a lot in the brewing of American mainstream beers, but they require cooking to gelatinize the starch. Flaked maize is obtained by moistening the grits with live steam and then passing them through heated rollers, which flatten them into flakes and gelatinize the starch. This means that the flakes can be added directly to the mash for starch conversion. In British practice, this is usually done at a rate of around 15% of the total grist.

Flaked maize must be mashed and cannot be used in malt extract brews unless you are using the partial-mash technique; in this case, it should be mashed along with the pale malt. It yields around 1.036 (9.0 °P)/pound/U.S. gallon and adds virtually nothing in the way of flavor or color and only a small amount of soluble nitrogen. I used it in my early brewing days simply because I was trying to emulate the commercial brewers. You will find its use recommended in many of the English homebrewing books of the 1970s and 1980s. For my part, it did not take long to decide that it did nothing for me, and I abandoned its use long before I moved to America.

Hops

The hop flower, whether used as such or in the form of hop pellets, is an essential brewing ingredient. It adds flavor from the bitterness it imparts, as well as aromatic qualities, which are usually characteristic of the particular hop employed. This is especially true of pale ale, which has always been a hop-centered beer. Here I discuss hop varieties and their selection for pale ale brewing, as well as the different hop products available and how they should be used.

Selecting Hops

Hops are the heart and soul of any pale ale. A definite hop bitterness is essential to the pale ale style in all of its forms. Hop flavor and character are by no means present in every example of the style. Further, there seems to be a trend to reduce these in English brewing, especially by the larger brewers. But when dealing with high levels of bitterness, it is easy to make a very one-dimensional beer, especially if it is brewed at a gravity below 1.040 (10.0 °P). Hop aroma and flavor give these beers greater complexity and interest—the better examples of the style usually have these attributes. Indeed, by definition, they should be present in American pale ales and IPAs.

If the hop is so important in pale ale brewing, how do you decide which is best suited for it? First, you select the variety you want for bitterness. That should be easy, shouldn't it, since you know that alpha acid is the determining factor in bitterness. So all you need is the hop with the highest level of alpha acid, right?

Not quite. The first point is that hops have a quality of bitterness—some hops give a harsher, less clean bitter flavor than others, even when bittering levels are identical. Second, there is some indication that the choice of bittering hops also affects hop flavor and aroma, even

A view of the exterior of the Cheriton brew house in Hampshire. A simple but functional building where they turn out some of the hoppiest bitters you can find.

though these characteristics come from the hop essential oils.[14] In theory, these oils should be lost during the boil, since bittering hops are added as boiling commences. But the chemistry of hop oils is complicated. It is possible that some volatile constituents could be converted into other compounds that might remain in the beer and affect its flavor.

That there appears to be qualitative differences in bitterness is very important. This is because bitterness levels are high in this style of beer, and any harsh flavors will be exaggerated, compared to many other styles. The drive toward the production of high alpha acid hop varieties has come from the major brewers of America and England. And these are the ones that tend to use quite low bittering levels, where qualitative differences in bitterness are unlikely to be noticeable.

Determining the likely bittering character of a particular hop variety is not easy. Attempts have been made to correlate this character with aspects of hop character and in particular the proportion of co-humulone. Co-humulone is one of the three major alpha acids. It does seem that a high level of it (30% or more of the total alpha acids) gives a harsh bitterness at relatively high bittering levels. Other factors such as wort pH might also play a major role here.[15] I am not sure I accept this approach. Some of the newer high alpha acid English hops, such as Phoenix and Progress, have high co-humulone levels (30% or more of total alpha acid), but they give clean bittering.[16]

There have also been approaches suggested for the selection of aroma hops based on analytical data of hop oil. For example, a humulene/caryophylline ratio of greater than three has been used to define noble hops.[17] An aroma unit (AU) has also been proposed that would be based on a profile of certain oil constituents, as determined by gas chromatography.[18]

This is perhaps academic to the craftbrewer, and certainly so to the homebrewer, as neither are likely to be able to perform the necessary analyses themselves. It might help, however, in selecting a particular variety using published analyses. This analytical approach also helps to point out the pitfalls in selecting a suitable hop variety for both bittering and aroma. In practice, it comes down to following the line on what has been traditionally found suitable for this type of beer. For example, Goldings and Fuggles, the so-called English noble hops, would be a first choice for an English bitter or IPA. First choice for an American pale ale, however, would undoubtedly be Cascades.

I do not want to get too deeply into the chemistry of hops here, as it is very complicated. As I have indicated, definitive conclusions cannot always be drawn from it. There is a good deal of information available in the literature (see appendix B). And once you have read all that you

TABLE 6

Hop Varieties in Pale Ale Brewing

Variety	Source	Alpha Acid %	Aroma/ Bittering	Suitable Beer
Fuggles	England[1]	4–5	Both	Bitter, PA, IPA
Goldings	England[2]	4–6	Both	PA, IPA
Target	England	10–13	Bittering	Bitter
Progress	England	5–8	Both	Bitter, IPA
Challenger	England	7–10	Both	Bitter, PA
Phoenix	England	8–12	Both	Bitter, PA
WGV[3]	England	5–7	Both	Bitter, IPA
Saaz	Czech Republic	4–5	Both	Bitter, PA, IPA
Styrian Goldings	Slovenia	4–6	Aroma	Bitter
Cascades	U.S.	4–7	Both	U.S. PA, IPA
Columbus	U.S.	10–13	Bittering	U.S. IPA
Mt. Hood[5]	U.S.	4–6	Aroma	Bitter, U.S. IPA
Liberty	U.S.	3–5	Aroma	PA, IPA
Willamette[4]	U.S.	3-6	Both	Bitter, PA, IPA
Crystal[5]	U.S.	3–5	Aroma	Bitter, U.S. IPA
Ultra[5]	U.S.	3–5	Aroma	Bitter, U.S. IPA
Centennial	U.S.	9–12	Both	U.S. PA, IPA
Chinook	U.S.	11–13	Bittering	Bitter
Northern Brewer[6]	U.S.	7–10	Bittering	Bitter, U.S. PA

[1]Also grown in America, but the English version is more aromatic and cleaner bittering.

[2]Also grown in British Columbia, but those are inferior to those grown in East Kent. For British brewers, this is *the* pale ale hop.

[3]Whitbread Goldings Variety; actually closely related to Fuggles.

[4]Related to Fuggles.

[5]German Hallertauer derivatives.

[6]Originally an English hop, now grown in both Germany and America. Popular with American brewers; regarded as somewhat coarse in England.

can read, then read the article by Jim Busch, "How to Master Hop Character." It outlines a good experimental approach to choosing hop varieties. An excellent article on the derivation of hop varieties and their relation to each other is "The Breeding and Parentage of Hop Varieties," by Gerard W. Ch. Lemmens. Both are cited in appendix B.

Here, I simply review some of the more commonly available varieties, with some typical analyses. I also offer recommendations regarding for which beer they are most suited. All of this information is summarized in table 6.

This review is somewhat subjective, representing only my opinion and practice. And it is by no means an exclusive list, for there are other good hops out there. There appears to be a trend in brewing circles to do something different, since "everybody does pale ale." But even the most dedicated brewer should never finish experimenting with pale ale. Hop flavors form such a large part of these beers, and there are so many different hops with so many different bittering and aroma characteristics.

You can, of course, use several different hop varieties in a single brew, and that is common commercial and amateur practice. It permits the use of high alpha acid hops for bittering and low alpha acid aroma hops for late hopping. Commercially, this makes sense, as it is the most economical use of the more expensive aroma hops. The savings are not significant to the home-brewer, however, and even the craftbrewer must balance such savings against the need to produce a beer of character and complexity.

My own approach for this type of beer is generally to use the low alpha acid aroma types for both bittering and aroma. Even the high alpha acid ones listed in table 6, such as Chinook, Centennial, and Northern Brewer, are considered by some brewers to give a somewhat unpleasant hop flavor. Others, such as Challenger, are high in alpha acid, yet they can also make a good aroma hop. Much of this choice is a matter of taste; for instance, I have one acquaintance who just cannot stand any beer brewed with Cascades.

One other interesting trend has developed in craft-brewing in America: the use of a single hop variety for all aspects of hop flavor. It started in English commercial brewing; even one of the big brewers, Whitbread, has come out with its Fuggles Imperial IPA that has even made its way to America.[19] I recommend this approach for all brewers, particularly those that want to learn to distinguish between different varieties. I have done it for many years with my own pale ales and IPAs, initially by way of experimentation, but I have stuck to it because I like the results.

My own choice for English bitters, and especially IPAs, is still the traditional Goldings and Fuggles. Both give a beautiful smooth bitterness and a definite citrus and delicate flowery character to these beers. In recent years, it seems that some of my best beers are those brewed with Fuggles. I have also had delightful results with Whitbread Goldings variety, which is why I included it in table 6, even though it is quite difficult to find in America. And I do like Cascades for my American-style pale ales, even though it can be somewhat overpowering!

Using Hops

But just choosing a hop variety is not enough. You also must decide what form you are going to use.

The main choice of form is between flowers and pellets; however, hop extracts and oils can also be used. For craftbrewers, the choice might be dictated by equipment concerns. If you have a hop back, you will probably want to stick with flowers. (I discuss the hop back further later in this chapter.) If you have a whirlpool for trub separation after the boil, pellets are the way to go.

Hop flowers. Good, fresh hop flowers, properly packed and stored, are hard to beat. They also are hard to handle, especially for the homebrewer. The resin glands are not uniformly distributed throughout the hops, and it is virtually impossible to sample them representatively when taking only an ounce or two at a time. Nor are they always stored properly by suppliers or by homebrewers. They tend to deteriorate more quickly than pellets, so their actual alpha acid content might be quite different from that stated on the label. This means, of course, that it is difficult to reach targeted bittering levels. So you need to be sure that your supplier is knowledgeable. If you have doubts about how he handles flowers, then either change your supplier or go with pellets.

Hop pellets. I think that the aroma from late hopping with pellets is as good as you can get with flowers (provided the latter are at their best). Pellets, in general, are easier to store and to handle. The argument against pellets is that they might have lost some of the hop oil in the compression process, and this argument does have some merit. However, hop pellets are somewhat more stable than flowers because they can be easily packaged securely. Also, they have greater uniformity, thereby allowing them to give more reproducible results in bittering. They further give better utilization of alpha acids, since the resin glands are ruptured during processing.

The most commonly available form is the Type 90 hop pellet. This is essentially whole flowers in pellet form. You can also get Type 45, which has much of the nonessential material removed and is consequently much higher in alpha acid. Also, a pre-isomerized pellet form is on the market, although not for homebrewers, as far as I am aware. I have not experimented with these, so I cannot say much about them.

Hop extracts. Hop extracts are also available. Mark Garetz, in his book *Using Hops*, considers that carbon dioxide extracts are the best.[2c] Pre-isomerized extracts can also be found and are useful for adjusting bitterness post-fermentation. The general opinion is that they do not provide bitterness of the same quality as hops added at the start of the boil. Factory brewers like them, but it has been suggested that they are not worthwhile for home- and craftbrewers.[21]

Hop oils. Finally, you also can obtain hop oil and even late hop essence. Both can be added to the beer at kegging, in place of dry hopping. These are made from only a few varieties. I have done a little experimentation with them but so far have not been impressed with the results.

Determining the Amount of Hops to Use

Determining the amount of hops needed to reach a particular level of bitterness is not always easy. Bitterness is expressed in IBUs (international bittering units), which is measured on the finished beer by a prescribed analytical, spectrophotometric method.[22] This method is not very suitable for homebrewers, few of whom own a spectrophotometer. Craftbrewers, however, might find it worthwhile to invest in a suitable instrument; if not, they should at least get a brewing laboratory to perform regular analyses for them.

Strictly speaking, the IBU value of a beer is just a number. However, it in fact closely approximates the level of iso-alpha-acids in mg/l (ppm), provided the hops are reasonably fresh. If this is the case, IBUs can be related to added alpha acids by the following equation:

$$IBU = \frac{G \times U \times a \times 0.1}{V}$$

where G is the weight of hops in grams, U is the percentage utilization of hop alpha acids (as a whole number), a is the percentage alpha acid in the hops (as a whole number), and V is the final beer volume, in liters.

This equation can be transposed into another version using the more common (and more unwieldy!) American units:

$$IBU = \frac{O \times U \times a \times 0.751}{V}$$

where U and a are the same as above, but O is the weight of hops in ounces, and V is the final beer volume in U.S. gallons.

This equation can easily be transposed to solve for the weight of hops of a given alpha acid content in order to achieve a given IBU in the beer. Although some consider this an "inaccurate" equation, it most definitely is not, for it is only the expression of the definition of IBU (yet there is more to bitterness than just IBU and alpha acid). The catch is that the data you put in is often inaccurate. You depend on the supplier's information for alpha acid values, and the value of the actual sample used differs from this, depending on storage and uniformity of sampling. And you do not know an accurate value for utilization unless you have determined it directly through an analysis of the beer.

Utilization depends on a whole range of factors. These include when the hops are added during the boil, the specific gravity of both the boil and the finished wort, fermentation temperatures, and so on. It is possible to make adjustments for these if you wish (see Mark Garetz's *Using Hops* and Michael Hall's "IBU" in appendix B). The calculations are fairly complicated, particularly if you are using different varieties that are added at different times during the boil.

I consider this equation useful because it serves as an approximation in reaching a desired bittering level. It also is useful for comparing different beers and for converting from one hop variety to another. The added level of calculation referred to previously might simply compound errors, since you still have to guess at alpha acid levels, as well as at losses with the trub and during fermentation. I simply make the assumption that the homebrewer will achieve 25% utilization, while the craftbrewer should expect approximately 30%. I also assume that all of the bittering hops are added at the beginning of the boil. Further, I ignore the contribution of aroma hops to bittering and that the boil is at least the full wort volume. Extract brewers boiling only a partial amount of the finished volume might want to allow for this, as described in the above references. Otherwise, I believe the only real alternative to using this equation is analysis of the finished beer.

There is an even simpler approach: using *alpha acid units* (AAUs), sometimes called *hop bitterness units* (HBUs). An AAU or HBU is simply the weight of hops in ounces multiplied by their percentage alpha acid. If you brew to the same finished volume each time, AAU or HBU can be useful for converting from one variety to another and for comparing different bittering rates; however, it has no absolute value. It can be misleading when brew volumes change. It might be better used in the form of volume alpha acid units (VAAUs), the weight of hops multiplied by alpha acid percentage divided by beer volume in U.S. gallons. Like all of these calculations, it can really be meaningful only if the alpha acid value you use is accurate.

Producing Hop Character in Pale Ales

Next, I address aroma and flavor hops. You can add these whenever and wherever you like in all pale ales. As I mentioned previously, at least some of the hop flavor comes from the bittering hops. An old German technique called first wort hopping has re-emerged recently. This technique calls for the aroma hops (usually noble hops) to be added to the wort before boiling. The result is reported as a pleasing, if unobtrusive, aroma to the beer.[23] I am not sure that this would be appropriate for a heavily hopped American pale ale, but I would be interested to hear from anyone trying it.

For more hop character, you can use the usual technique of a late addition with good quality aroma hops. This might mean adding hops 15 to 20 minutes before the end of the boil, just at the end of the boil, or into the hop back. The hop back, sometimes also called a "jack," is a device for straining off spent hops. It is a very old-style piece of equipment but is still used by a number of English traditional brewers and by some American craftbrewers. The homebrewer can construct a similar device by using a fairly coarse mesh strainer, such as a sanitized piece of nylon window screen. Add the aroma hops to the screen, and then run the hot wort through it before cooling. Take care to avoid splashing the wort, or the aeration this causes might result in oxidation problems in the beer. This technique is suitable only if you are using whole hop flowers. It clearly will not work well with pellets and is not for craftbrewers who use a whirlpool in place of a hop back.

Achieving hop aroma in a beer by late hopping is not easy for the homebrewer. This is because the surface area to volume ratio is several orders of magnitude higher for a 5-gallon brew than it is for a 5-barrel volume. As a result, the volatile hop oils are much more readily lost on the smaller scale. You might have to use at least two or three times as much aroma hops as the professional brewer in order to get similar results. Often this might mean that, on the basis of weight, you need to add more aroma hops than bittering hops.

Since you are going to conduct a relatively warm fermentation, the combination of temperature and foaming results in the loss of much of the hop aroma added by late hopping methods. To get more aroma into the beer, you might have to resort to dry hopping. In traditional English practice, this means adding some hops in flower form to the cask right after the beer is racked. As the beer conditions in the cask, it adsorbs the flavor of the hops. The beer is cool compared to hot wort, so the flavoring components of the hops are taken up virtually unchanged. This gives the beer an aromatic character unobtainable by more normal late hopping methods. Dry hopping is still done by English brewers, although usually only with cask-conditioned beers, not with pasteurized, artificially carbonated beers. Dry hopping can also be accomplished during conditioning, prior to filtration.

Dry hopping in the fermenter is sometimes practiced in America. Some brewers use it in the primary, but this can cause problems, particularly if you use a blow-off type of system, where blockage of the blow-off tube can occur. It is probably better to do this in the secondary, which more closely approaches dry hopping of cask-conditioned beer. But simply adding hops to the fermenter, whether flower or pellets, might make racking difficult. The best approach is to use a hop bag that is weighted down to prevent it from floating (the weight, of course, must be carefully sanitized before use).

The form of late or dry hops is a matter of choice, as in bittering hop selection. Flower hops can cause processing difficulties. This is because they are a challenge to separate from the beer. They also will readily block any sort of tube, such as a racking cane, or the outlet of the type of stainless steel soda keg, which is often used for draught beer by the homebrewer. Pellets present less difficulty in this respect but might not give the same aromatic character as flower hops because of how they are processed.

Clearly, you have to use top-quality hops, regardless of how or when you add them. You can use some of the high alpha acid hops, but these often contribute very harsh flavors. In general, it is better to stick to the classic aroma hop types, such as Goldings and Fuggles and their derivatives, the noble hops Saaz, Hallertauer and its relatives, and so on (see table 6 for my recommendations). These might be more expensive, but you really do not want to spoil the beer by worrying about cost at this stage of the proceedings.

The whole business of achieving hop flavor and aroma is very much an art. It is difficult to obtain consistent results with any of the previous approaches, even for the craftbrewer. This is probably why the major factory brewers have tried to eliminate these aspects of beer character from their products. For them, consistency is everything; for us, unpredictability is a delight! Experimentation with the choice and point of addition of aroma hops leads us into an amazing spectrum of beers. A pale ale full of bitterness, hop character, and aroma is a wonderfully complex brew—satisfying, enjoyable, intriguing, and a pleasure in every glass.

Yeast

It is often said that there are two major types of yeasts: top-fermenting and bottom-fermenting. Pale ale must be made with a top-fermenting yeast. But what exactly does this mean?

Types of Yeast

First, let me be clear: fermentation does not take place on the surface of the beer. It is the yeast suspended *in* the beer that does the work. It is only after the major part of the fermentation is over that the yeast begins to separate from suspension. When it does so, either it rises to the surface or it sediments. This is where the traditional nomenclature of top-fermenting and bottom-fermenting derives.

But modern commercial brewers often use closed, conical fermenters, in which every type of yeast settles at the bottom. And indeed, quite a few strains of "top-fermenting yeasts" do not migrate to the surface, but rather sediment like bottom-fermenting yeasts. Many yeasts available to the homebrewer, especially those supplied with malt extracts or kits, fit this category, since the manufacturer wants to make sure his customer brews clear beer. At one time, a distinction was made between the two types by taxonomists: top-fermenting yeast was termed *Saccharomyces cerevisiae*, and bottom-fermenting *Saccharomyces uvarum*. However, both are now classified as belonging to the same subfamily, *Saccharomyces cerevisiae*. [24]

The terms *top-fermenting* and *bottom-fermenting* have been used for over a century. Top-fermenting yeast was collected by skimming it from the top of the beer in ale brewing, and bottom-fermenting yeast was collected from the bottom of the fermenter in lager brewing. This was a crude form of yeast selection, or culturing, that led to the elimination of strains that did not suit the method of collection. Consequently, yeasts are better distinguished by the type of beer to which they are best suited and by the fermentation temperatures appropriate to each type of beer. Ale yeasts give optimum results at temperatures in the range 60–70 °F (15.6–21.1 °C) and usually stop fermenting as the temperature approaches 50 °F (10 °C). They might separate on the surface at the end of primary fermentation. Lager yeasts, on the other hand, ferment well at temperatures below 50 °F (10 °C) and sediment to the bottom of the fermenter.

The warmer fermentation temperatures of ales result in the formation of a number of chemical compounds that are not generally seen in lagers. Since most of these are of an aromatic nature (in sensory, rather than chemical terms!), lagers are generally held to result in a cleaner, smoother drink. In fact, these fermentation by-products help to give pale ale its complexity and character. Chief among these are the various esters (compounds of acids and alcohols), which are detectable by their fruity aromas and flavors.

There is more to this than temperature, however, for some yeast strains produce more esters than others do under similar conditions. The yeast used by Sierra Nevada for its pale ale, for example, is renowned for its clean fermentation characteristics because it produces few esters. Many of the yeasts used by English brewers give significant amounts of esters and produce fruity beers; the Ringwood strain (used by many microbrewers) is a good example. And, in fact, many English brewing yeasts are a combination of several strains, although this is now perhaps less often the case than previously.

Individual ale yeast strains can have very different fermentation characteristics in terms of attenuation of wort sugars. You need a high-attenuating strain if you want to re-create one of the early IPAs. A low-attenuating one is more suited to a beer such as an ESB, in which a maltier character is desired. Attenuation depends in part on the flocculation characteristics of the strain. *Flocculation* is the ability of the yeast to aggregate, or clump together, at the end of the first fermentation stage. High-flocculating yeasts settle out very readily and might do so before attenuation is complete. Low-flocculating yeasts separate much less readily and so often give quite complete attenuation. This has led to the design of different types of fermenters, such as Burton Unions, Yorkshire stone squares, and so on, in order to get the desired attenuation from a strain that gives suitable flavors.

Types of Fermenters

The vessels you have in part decide what strains of yeast you can use. Conical fermenters are the most versatile because they permit the use of virtually any strain, whether sedimenting or not. The glass carboys favored by so many homebrewers also permit the use of a wide range of strains, but they work best with sedimenting types. True top-fermenting yeasts do not work well in carboys, unless handled by the blow-off technique. This technique consists of using a stopper drilled to take a wide tube that leads into a collecting vessel. During the early stages of fermentation, when vigorous frothing occurs, a lot of foam is pushed out into the collector and must be discarded. Note, this technique has been called a Burton Union type of system, but it most certainly is not. The Burton Union system calls for the return of the collected beer after the separation of the yeast. In its original concept, it was not used for the early stages of fermentation, which were performed in a standard open vessel. In the blow-off system, the overflow beer is simply lost. Hop bittering resins are surface-active materials and are lost with the foam. This does not help the head formation characteristics of the finished beer. There also is a risk of blockage of the blow-off tube, thereby resulting in a very dangerous situation because of the high pressures that can then develop in the vessel. In my view, the blow-off system has little to recommend it. It is better to use an oversized carboy, with 1 to 2 gallons of headspace above the beer, and to rack into a smaller vessel as soon as the primary fermentation subsides.

Other closed vessels are available to the homebrewer. These include a conical fermenter, constructed of plastic, as well as several kits that permit the inversion of a carboy, with a cap that allows both yeast collection and pressure relief. Conical fermenters can be unwieldy, and the yeast often does not flow well through the collection tubes prior to racking. But I have had satisfactory results with this type of closed vessel. My own approach is to use a 7-gallon polycarbonate vessel, fitted with a lid that can take a fermentation lock, and a bottom take-off tap. This makes for easy racking and copes nicely with true top-fermenting yeasts, which are simply left on the bottom of the vessel at racking.

Traditional English brewers still often use an open fermenter and swear that it is the only way to get the best flavors in a cask-conditioned bitter. In the simplest open fermenter, the beer is held until ready for casking, at which time it is transferred from the fermenter to a racking back. To use an open fermenter properly, you must have a yeast that will form a good thick skin on the surface. This skin acts as a protective layer for the beer once the violent stage of fermentation is over. Open fermentation is practiced by some American craftbrewers, particularly those that have installed British-designed equipment. It is not a technique that homebrewers like much, however, partly because it is difficult to obtain the right type of yeast and partly because the risk of infection is higher than with a closed vessel.

Open fermenters, called "rounds" at one time because of their round shape, used to be wooden and lined with copper for ease of cleaning. Rectangular construction in stainless steel is now more common. Fermenters of this type are usually quite shallow, much more so than conical vessels. I do not discuss the details of fermenter construction here, particularly the more complicated Burton Union and Yorkshire stone square systems, although both are still used in England. For a good, general account of this, see Michael J. Lewis and Tom W. Young's *Brewing* cited in appendix B.

Affect of Temperature on Yeast

In the fermentation of pale ales, warm temperatures are used, normally 65–70 °F (18.3–21.1 °C). A good deal of heat is generated during fermentation. Commercial brewers control this temperature by cooling (attemperation) by using either cold water coils in the vessel or a cooling jacket. If the temperature rises much above 70 °F (21.1 °C), the yeast will produce more esters, as well as fusel oils. Although esters might be an important part of the pale ale flavor spectrum, you can have too much of a good thing.

Unfortunately, maintaining the temperature of fermentation in this temperature region is not always easy for the amateur, especially in summer. However, it might not be so difficult as it at first seems. A 5-gallon brew has a significantly higher surface-to-volume ratio than does a vessel taking several barrels or more, so it will dissipate heat much more readily than is the case on a commercial scale. As long as the ambient temperature is about right, you should have no problems with the heat generated in fermentation. However, note that fermenting in glass does not help, since glass is a fairly good insulator. If outside temperatures are much higher than 70 °F (21.1 °C), you either have to abandon brewing or find some way to cool the fermenter. This can be done by either immersing it in cold water, covering it with wet towels, or whatever.

Choosing a Yeast Strain

The choice of yeast is of paramount importance, and the availability of yeast varieties is something that has changed dramatically since my first book on pale ale. There is now a very wide range of yeasts available to both the amateur and the professional. They come in three basic forms—dry, liquid, and slant—and from a number of suppliers. For a complete listing of all yeast strains, consult the "Yeast Directory" in the *Brewers Market Guide* (published annually by New Wine Press), which quotes over 80 strains for English ale styles alone. Although this guide is very comprehensive, it does not list the strains in the English National Yeast Culture Collection (held at the Food Research Institute, Colony Lane, Norwich, England NR4 7UA).

An extensive article on yeast by Patrick Weix (listed in appendix B) is aimed at the homebrewer. It gives the homebrewer (as well as the craftbrewer) a whole new perspective for a pale ale, a beer style that may have anything from nothing to a great deal of character supplied by the yeast. It also offers you the possibility of matching some of your favorite commercial beers, if that is what you want. However, there is little to define an individual yeast strain, and when they have been obtained from brewers originally, the brewer's name is never supplied. You have to make do with terms such as *Irish ale* or with simply a set of numbers. The suppliers will offer you information about ester production, attenuation levels, and degree of flocculation. But this information is simply a guide; you have to experiment to find out what suits you best. There is not a lot of information in the brewing literature on individual strains. However, George and Laurie Fix give some excellent information on a limited number of them in their book *An Analysis of Brewing Techniques*.[25]

There is now no need for the kit brewer to accept the pack of dried yeast that comes with his purchase. Not that there is necessarily anything wrong with the offerings of individual kits. But you usually have no idea of the source or the viability of these yeasts, although the quality of dried yeast has improved immeasurably in recent years. Today, a relatively small number of brewery strains are available. For example, the Whitbread strain from G. W. Kent's yeast lab has given me excellent results in the past, with good attenuation and rapid flocculation resulting in a dry, slightly fruity beer. However, I have read that this strain might no longer attenuate as well as it once did.[26] Other dried yeasts that I have had good results with include Lallemand's Nottingham and London strains. My favorite is not available in America—it is the dried brewing yeast sold by Boot's, an English pharmacist. It is an excellent fast starter, gives high attenuation (78–80%) and moderate esters, but settles out rather slowly, unless fined with *isinglass*, a substance used to flocculate yeast in cask-conditioned beer. If any retailer is looking to expand his range of dried yeasts, I recommend this one.

Although you can get away with adding modern dried yeasts directly to the wort, I recommend making a starter by adding a couple of 5-gram packets to a pint of previously prepared and cooled wort. Prepare it a couple of days before brewing so that when the high kraeusen in your starter begins to subside, the wort is ready for pitching. This allows you to ensure that you have a viable yeast before you start brewing, as well as sufficient active yeast to get your fermentation quickly under way, with little risk of infection occurring.

The major advance for the homebrewer and craftbrewer is the wide range of strains available as liquids or culture slants. These are a little more difficult to use, as they must be built up as a starter. Begin with, say, one-quarter of a pint of wort, and add this to a pint when it is at full kraeusen. Then increase the wort to 1 quart, and even to a full half-gallon, before pitching to your 5 gallons of wort. The difficulty here is that you must observe maximum cleanliness in doing this step-up so that you do not add an infected starter to your beer. This sounds like quite a bit of effort, and it does require some planning and preparation. But this process makes such a wide range of yeasts and different flavors available to you that it is well worth trying. There are several articles and books, listed in appendix B, that discuss this in more detail.

You can, of course, culture your own yeast, especially if you are able to obtain strains otherwise not available on the market. I do not deal with that here because of space constraints, but most of the references in appendix B contain sufficient information for homebrewers. Craft-brewers should also monitor the quality of their yeast, since it is not only their lifeblood, but also potentially their Achilles heel. Even the major brewers have been known to have yeast infection problems—these can cause both lost batches and lost customers. A relatively small investment in a microscope and a few petri dishes can save significant amounts of money in the long run.[27]

The simplest approach is the use of the so-called "smack packs." A smack pack is a small pouch of yeast contained inside a larger one that holds a nutrient solution. You simply smack the pack to break the yeast pouch; you know the yeast is viable and ready when the outer pouch swells. Many homebrewers pitch this directly into the wort, but this is really an insufficient amount of yeast for a rapid take-off of fermentation. For best results, you should still make, say, a 1-quart starter from this pack.

For a rapid, complete fermentation, you need not only a good, active starter and a sufficient yeast count for a successful fermentation, but also a well-oxygenated wort. Craftbrewers and some homebrewers have turned to direct oxygenation of the chilled wort, rather than the more common practice of aeration through agitation and "splashing" from one vessel to another.[28] This is a good approach to total control of fermentation and one the craftbrewer in particular should carefully consider. I have

TABLE 7

Yeast Suggestions

Strain	Source	Esters	Flocculence[1]	Beer Substyle
1028 London Ale[2]	Wyeast	Moderate	High	Best and ordinary bitter, IPA
1187 Ringwood	Wyeast	Moderate to high	Medium[3]	Bitters, American ambers
CL-120 British Pale Ale #1[4]	Brew Tek	Moderate to high	Medium	Pale ale, IPA
CL-240 Irish Dry Stout[5]	Brew Tek	Moderate[6]	Medium	Special bitters, American amber
Microbrewery Ale[7]	Brew Tek	Low	Medium high	American pale ales and IPAs
Y29 Triple Pack Ale[8]	Williams	Moderate	Medium	Bitters, pale ales
1968 London ESB[9]	Wyeast	Moderate to high	High	Special bitters

[1]This is a relative term and might indicate a fast-settling yeast or one that forms a good skin. The yeasts mentioned here almost all give high attenuation when properly handled.

[2]While it has been suggested that this is a Burton Ale yeast, my own comparison with a Young's yeast obtained elsewhere indicates that the London Ale designation is correct. *Source:* George J. Fix and Laurie A. Fix, *An Analysis of Brewing Techniques* (Boulder, Colo.: Brewers Publications, 1997), 62.

[3]This can, and often does, give the beer a very complex estery character, which can be too much for some tastes!

[4]This does in fact seem to be a Burton Ale. As such, it warrants trying by all pale ale brewers at least once.

[5]This is probably a Guinness yeast and, though obviously meant for stout, works very well in English pale ales and American ambers. These cultures do not seem to work as well as those I could once get from bottle-conditioned Guinness in England that gave amazing kraeusen and skin formation!

[6]This yeast often gives moderately high levels of diacetyl. As long as this is not overdone, it can add a nice edge of complexity to a special bitter.

[7]Basically, the yeast for Sierra Nevada, yielding a clean, relatively neutral flavor.

[8]This might no longer be available. It is very interesting as one of the few deliberately produced mixed cultures.

[9]This ostensibly is Fuller's ESB yeast and therefore mandatory to try if you want to produce something in the full, fruity, strong bitter style.

found it unnecessary to oxygenate my worts, relying instead on thorough agitation and the use of a good volume of active starter culture.

Can I recommend any good cultures for beers in the pale ale style? I am reluctant to do this because so many of the strains available are proprietary and so many exist that I have been unable to try them all. Table 7 lists some suggestions on strains that have given me good results.

Please, please do not see table 7 as limiting your choice of yeast. First, other suppliers than those mentioned probably offer something similar and so should not be ignored. Second, I have not by any means tried all of the yeasts available on the market. I tend to keep a good one going when I find it, and some of my successes have been with yeasts that I have obtained privately and that are just not available in America. And do remember that the choice of yeast for a particular beer might be a compromise. Something that gives a good flavor profile might not give the attenuation you want or might cause problems with clarification. But yeast is a rich field in which to experiment. The various American suppliers are to be congratulated on their offerings. They have done a good job of supplying a wide range of ale yeasts, much better than their English counterparts, especially as far as the homebrewer is concerned.

Water

It is a truism to say that the quality of brewing water is of paramount importance in brewing good beer. But the one thing you do not want is pure water. Instead, you want water that contains a suitable salt content to give the desired results. This means that the water should have the right *kind* of salts so that the mash pH (acidity) is in the range 5.2–5.5. In this way, you can obtain optimum performance from the malt enzymes and therefore maximum starch conversion. For pale ales, in which the main grain is pale ale malt, which is low in acidity, this means that you do not want an alkaline water. In particular, you do not want one that is high in bicarbonate, or temporary hardness. If it is, you can compensate by adjusting salt content through adding acidic salts such as calcium sulfate (gypsum).

But do you really need to do this? It is well known that most of the great brewing styles came into being because the places where they were brewed had just the right water for that particular style. Pilsen has soft water suited to pale lagers; London and Dublin have relatively alkaline waters suited to the brewing of dark beers, such as porters and stouts; and Burton has very hard water that is high in calcium and sulfate and is just perfect for pale ales. Yet these reputations for certain beer styles brewed in certain places came about only a hundred or more years ago, when malt quality was not what it is today. Today, it is much easier to be careless about mash pH and still get good conversion than was the case in the early nineteenth century. And if you brew from malt extract, there is no need to add salts to adjust mash pH, since the mashing has already been done for you.

I am not suggesting that you should simply ignore water quality and plough ahead, just that you should not perhaps be overly concerned about it. If the water contains no nasties such as bacteria or organic material and is fit to drink, try a mash and check its pH. If the pH is in the right region, you can proceed with brewing; if not, try adding gypsum in small increments until you bring the acidity into the range cited previously. Note how much gypsum you have added, and add the same amount in future brews—you should be all right (although it would be wise to check the pH at each mash). If the gypsum addition does not correct the pH, then you do have a problem and must do something about it.

However, there is more to water than just mash acidity. Certain salts will have an effect on beer flavor, and their addition might be desirable on those grounds alone. For the purposes of brewing pale ales and bitters, where hop bitterness is such an important flavor component, the sulfate ion is essential because it enhances bitterness. Too much sulfate can lead to a harsh bitterness, however, so the presence of chloride ions can be useful also, as these tend to mellow and soften the beer. Too much bicarbonate can make it difficult to adjust mash pH, as well as possibly cause the beer to have a flat, flabby flavor spectrum.

I do not want to go into great detail here, as the chemistry of water is amazingly complex and has already been well covered in the literature (see appendix B). I do recommend that you obtain a water analysis. This can be performed by either your water company if you are on a mains supply or a local laboratory if you are using a well.

If your water is high in organics and chlorine, then you might have to use an activated carbon filter. If it is high in certain metals, such as over 10 ppm (mg/l) copper and iron or high in nitrites, you might want to consider an ion exchange treatment. This must be of the two-stage cation/anion exchange. The single-stage cation exchange, used for water softening in household set-ups, will not yield good results. It simply replaces calcium with sodium—this is definitely not suitable for brewing purposes. For craftbrewers who want to brew several different styles from a water that is high in mineral content, ion exchange followed by salt adjustment for particular styles is a good, if relatively expensive, way to go.

You should remove chlorine because it can react with all kinds of beer organic components to give all types of beer off-flavors. If you do not use activated carbon for this, then at least boil the water first. Boiling is also a good way to reduce excessive levels of carbonate, which will precipitate as insoluble calcium carbonate. Note, however, that boiling removes only chlorine and not chloramines, which are often used in place of chlorine by water companies.

What does the rest of the water analysis tell you? It *will not* tell you which salts have been dissolved in the water. Rather, it will list only the ions present, which are positive (cations) and negative (anions). How do you use this information to ensure that your mash will be in the desired acidity range? There are equations you can use that will give a prediction of mash pH, but I have not used them.[29] I prefer the simpler approach of adjusting the ion content to what I think is suitable by adding salts. I find it simpler because I can work in direct ion concentrations and can avoid getting lost in the maze of different definitions of "hardness." I have to admit, however, that this is easy for me because my water is fairly soft, with a relatively low dissolved ion content. It is always easier to increase ion concentrations than it is to decrease them. In fact, the only way to reduce ion content, apart from removing carbonate and some excess iron by boiling, is by dilution with distilled water. That, of course, would reduce the concentrations of all ions present, in proportion to the dilution ratio.

To adjust the concentrations of the various ions, you have to know what your target is. This is not quite so simple. One approach is to look at the composition of a water you know to be suitable for brewing pales, and of course Burton water is an obvious candidate. Table 8 shows an analysis of Burton water, focusing on the typical values for the ions of most concern to brewers.

TABLE 8

Burton Brewing Water Analysis

Ion	Concentration mg/l (ppm)[*]
Calcium, Ca^{++}	270–300
Magnesium, Mg^{++}	20–40
Sodium, Na^+	20–30
Bicarbonate, HCO_3^-	200–250
Sulfate, SO_4^{--}	450–700
Chloride, Cl^-	35–40

[*]I have given a range here. There are many published analyses of Burton water, and there is some variation in their results due to variations in samples and analytical techniques.

A simple and effective method to produce a water suitable for brewing pale ales is to concentrate on the calcium and sulfate levels. Adjust these by adding gypsum to bring the concentrations of these ions in line with the data in table 8. I ignore magnesium because I do not consider that it has a significant effect at these calcium levels. (Also, I cannot forget that magnesium sulfate is a laxative!) If desired, you can also add sodium chloride to increase the levels of these two ions, although their concentration is quite low in table 8. In general, you do not want to add carbonate ions, unless your water is very, very soft. In the latter case, you can add calcium carbonate to increase the bicarbonate concentration. Note that calcium carbonate must be added to the mash, not the water, because it is not directly soluble in water. The best approach is to check mash pH and add calcium carbonate only if the pH is below 5.5. Then follow with plenty of agitation to ensure equilibrium is reached.

When adding salts, you might find the following equation helpful. Gypsum is $CaSO_4 \cdot 2H_2O$, so that

1 g gypsum/U.S. gallon
    = 61.5 mg /l calcium, 147.4 mg /l sulfate.

Sodium chloride (NaCl) is added as non-iodized table salt:

  1 g NaCl/U.S. gallon
  	= 104 mg /l sodium, 160 mg /l chloride.

Calcium carbonate, used as precipitated chalk $CaCO_3$, will give

  1 g CaCO3/U.S. gallon
  	= 106 mg /l calcium, 161 mg /l bicarbonate.

You can see that water treatment is not quite so simple as might be expected. Every salt you add puts two ions into solution, so exact balancing of every ion becomes almost impossible. This is why many brewers making this kind of adjustment add only gypsum in order to give a sufficient level of sulfate and calcium, in a process called burtonization. Sulfate is needed to adjust pH and for flavor reasons. Calcium is important in the brewing process for a variety of reasons—from buffering of the mash pH to helping to ensure good break formation and yeast flocculation. As you can see, it takes very little sodium chloride or calcium carbonate to increase the levels of chloride and bicarbonate to those found in Burton water.

TABLE 9

Targets for Pale Ale Brewing Water

Ion	Concentration mg/l (ppm)
Calcium	100–200
Magnesium	10–20
Sodium	10–20
Bicarbonate	50 maximum
Sulfate	200–500
Chloride	20–40

The problem with all of this is that Burton water is quite unique. It has a very high ion concentration and a very high level of dissolved solids (around 1,200 mg/l). The level of sulfate is extremely high, which is probably why the high level of bicarbonate is not a problem in brewing. It also leads to a so-called "sulfury" flavor to which I have referred earlier in chapter 1. In fact, it is more likely a combining of the mineral flavor of the sulfate with that of the high level of hops.[30] All in all, it can be argued that Burton water is so complex and unusual that you are better off not attempting to match it exactly and sticking to adding gypsum in most cases.

In general, I use a much simpler approach and try to hit some simple target ranges like those listed in table 9.

I would look to the lower end of these ranges for sulfate and calcium for a special bitter in which I wanted a more malty character. The same would apply if I were using an aggressively flavored hop like Cascades. If I wanted to soften a very high level of bitterness (say above 40 IBU), I might also go higher on the sodium chloride. However, I would limit it to a maximum of around 30 mg/l sodium and 60 mg/l chloride. As mentioned previously, there is a good argument for not getting too involved in the complexities of water treatment. If your supply gives a satisfactory pH for mashing, if extract efficiency is acceptable, and if the final result is a good beer, that is all you need to worry about.

Note that if you do treat the water, then you must do it to all of your brewing water, including that used for sparging. Otherwise, you might leach tannins from the malt husks during sparging. The result will be a beer with an unpleasant astringent flavor.

If you are brewing from extract, then you might want to make adjustments purely for flavor purposes. This should be done at the boil; all you need to do is to add a little gypsum. Add only 5–10 grams (1–2 teaspoonfuls, if you must be so crude!), and stir it thoroughly into the cooled wort. Do not add it to the hot wort, as gypsum has the unusual characteristic of being less soluble in a hot aqueous medium than in a cold one.

One last point in this age of "designer" water. If your supply does not appear to be suitable for brewing pale ales, be careful about using bottled spring water. Do get a full analysis of the water and check it carefully because if it is genuine spring water, it might well be unusually high in bicarbonate and not at all appropriate for pale ale. You might be better off looking into techniques such as ion exchange on your original supply or obtaining brewing water from an entirely different source.

CHAPTER 4

Packaging and Dispensing Methods

Aging

So, you have brewed the beer, and the primary fermentation is done. What next? There are no hard and fast rules, of course, but your approach is dictated by whatever substyle you are brewing. If you are making a low-gravity bitter, then it is perfectly possible to rack it directly into a cask or keg immediately after the primary fermentation is done. It is possible, but I do not recommend it.

For all pale ales, it is best to rack after primary and to hold in either a closed vessel or one fitted with a fermentation lock for from one to seven days. You can dry hop at this point if you wish, although traditionally this takes place in the cask. Racking after primary fermentation is beneficial because the beer does not sit on the dead yeast for any length of time; yeast allowed to do this can cause the development of off-flavors through autolysis. Also, the period of secondary fermentation, or conditioning, allows a reduction in yeast content so that the beer is ready for packaging. If you have too high a yeast content after the secondary fermentation, then you will have a lot of sediment in bottle-conditioned beer, difficulties in fining a cask-conditioned beer, or problems in filtration.

In fact, not much does occur in the way of secondary fermentation. With a good, healthy yeast added in sufficient quantity, all but the strongest of these beers should be down to finishing gravity at the end of primary fermentation. Also, it is not wise to cool the beer too soon, as a short period at relatively warm temperatures (60–70 °F, 15.6–21.1 °C) will ensure that diacetyl concentrations are at acceptable levels. Although these styles can stand more in the way of diacetyl than would be permissible in a pale lager, you will regret it if the levels are too high!

For a beer with an original gravity of up to 1.050 (12.4 °P) or so, you do not really need more than one week in the secondary. Long maturation times in the secondary or in the final container do not add anything to the flavor of this type of beer and will result in a loss of freshness. These beers are high in both hop bitterness and hop character; long storage causes a loss of both and will spoil the beer's impact. Possibly worse, if you have not excluded all air from your fermenter, bottle, or keg, then hop-derived compounds will oxidize, thereby giving a whole host of unpleasant-tasting products. Think fresh! In my opinion, lower-gravity bitters are best drunk within a week or so of kegging or casking. Special bitters, American pale ales, and amber ales will keep for a few more weeks, but do not overdo it.

IPAs, however, are a little different. Because of their higher gravities, they might not ferment fully in the primary and might need a few weeks in the secondary to reach full attenuation. Since they have very high levels of hop bitterness, they might taste quite harsh when just a week or two old; several months' maturation will help to smooth out the beer. Again, if you do not rigidly exclude air, such maturation might cause more problems than it cures.

If you want an oak flavor in your beer, consider maturing over oak chips. Lengthy maturation in wooden casks will not normally give an oak flavor, unless the type of oak has been carefully chosen to do just that. I discuss this a little further in this chapter under cask conditioning. I do not believe that oak should be a part of this beer's flavor spectrum, whatever might be said about Ballantine's IPA. It is certainly not a characteristic of any English beer that I have tasted and, as I discussed in chapter 1, probably did not apply to any of the pale ales of the nineteenth century.

In fact, long storage of pale ales results in a loss of hop bitterness and hop character. This might not be serious at higher bittering levels. I have kept bottles of my version of Original IPA (see chapter 1) for up to two years and could not detect any loss in bitterness. However, that beer could have been as high as 200 IBUs so that even a 50% reduction over two years would still have left it a very bitter beer by normal standards.

An issue I did not discuss in chapter 3 is finishing gravity, although I referred to it earlier in this chapter. With proper yeast management, you should be able to come very close to finishing gravity by the end of primary fermentation, no more than 0.002 points (about 0.5 °P) above your target. This applies even to the higher-gravity IPAs (close to 1.070, 17.1 °P). This is generally considered not true for high-gravity beers because ale yeasts supposedly have a relatively low alcohol tolerance. However, it has been well-demonstrated that beer yeasts are just as tolerant of high-alcohol concentrations as are wine yeasts.[1]

Clarifying Beer with Finings

Finings is a fine piece of brewer's jargon, if you will forgive the pun. Essentially, the term is applied to any additive that helps to clarify the beer. An example is copper finings, which are added to the kettle to flocculate the break.

Copper finings are actually called Irish moss, which in America largely comes from Massachusetts.[2] Irish moss contains carrageenan. Carrageenan is a complex mixture of polysaccharides, some of which carry acidic sulfate groups (a relatively unusual group in naturally occurring organic compounds). These groups neutralize the positively charged protein fragments that form the break, agglomerating them into larger particles that settle better than the small break particles. The idea behind using these is to get clear wort that contains very little trub and to reduce the risk of chill haze formation in the finished beer. However, it seems that some trub present in the wort might actually help yeast growth. For a 5-gallon brew volume, you need only 1–2 grams (a *pinch* is the term often used in the homebrewing literature).

I used Irish moss for several years, regarding it as small insurance to pay for a sound fermentation and a good clear beer. However, I had a problem with one batch of wort: It formed a very voluminous, fluffy break that was difficult to remove. In subsequent batches, I stopped using Irish moss, and I since have encountered no problems with either fermentation or final beer clarity.

In English brewing, the term *finings* is specifically applied to isinglass. Isinglass is prepared from the swim bladders of certain fish and is mainly collagen, a proteinaceous material.[3] Gelatin is similar but is much lower in molecular weight. Both substances carry negative and positive charges that are capable of binding with oppositely charged sites on the yeast wall. Yeast cell walls carry charges (usually positive), and these charges cause the yeast particles to repel each other so that they stay in suspension. The finings adsorb onto the cell wall, neutralizing the charges on the wall to enable the yeast particles to aggregate and form flocs. Large flocs settle out much more quickly than small flocs. The settling rate is roughly proportional to the square of the particle size. In other words, if one floc is 10 times bigger than another, it will settle at 100 times the speed of the smaller floc.

Isinglass is significantly higher in molecular weight than gelatin, so it carries more charge per molecule and is capable of forming much larger flocs than gelatin. This means that it will form a dense, compact sediment that is not easily disturbed in transit or when the beer is drawn off from the container. Isinglass will also pull out some proteins—this helps prevent haze formation and also contributes to the stability of beer foam.[4]

Gelatin is not used by many professional brewers because it is relatively slow acting. It offers no great advantage with well-flocculating yeast and has difficulty handling powdery yeasts. It is of some use to the home-brewer, however, simply because it is easier to handle than isinglass. For 5 gallons of beer, dissolve one standard sachet (0.5 ounce, 14 g) in warm, but not boiling, water, mix well with a pint of beer, and add it to the bulk of the beer. The gelatin might take several days or more to clear and cannot handle high levels of yeast at all. It is useful only for draught beers, since bottled beers will usually clear well if left alone. Even with draught beers, gelatin does not give much more of a compact sediment than can be obtained by natural settling of the yeast. And if you are going to keep the beer for a week or more before drinking anyway, the extra effort of adding gelatin hardly seems worthwhile.

Isinglass is much different. Properly used, it will make the beer fall bright within 24 hours. It will do so even if added at the brewery before shipping to an account. It has been used in England since the eighteenth century and is still preferred by many traditional brewers. It is not necessary if you centrifuge or plan to filter the green beer. But if you want to make a cask-conditioned beer, isinglass finings ensure bright beer that has a sediment that is not easily disturbed, even when the last few pints of beer in the cask are pumped off.

There are problems with isinglass, however, not the least of which is storage stability. Its big collagen molecule, so effective at clearing the beer, very quickly degrades at temperatures of 70 °F (21 °C); from that point, it is useless as a finings agent. Further, yeast count must be fairly well controlled, generally in the region of 1–2 million cells/milliliter. If it is much above or below this level, the beer might not clear well. In addition, not all yeasts respond well to isinglass (or other finings); its use should be restricted to English-style, top-fermenting strains. And if you get it wrong the first time, you cannot re-fine—the situation will just get worse.

Despite this, isinglass finings are not all that difficult to use, with a little care. The results are excellent, even for the homebrewer. This is especially true if soda kegs are used, since these are quite tall and the yeast has to fall a much greater distance than in, for example, a 12-ounce bottle. The result is that the beer can take a long time to clear on its own. I use soda kegs all of the time for my draught beers, and they are clear and ready to drink within a day or so after kegging or casking.

Do not buy liquid finings unless they have been kept refrigerated and you are taking them straight home. If finings must be shipped to you, then the liquid form will almost certainly have degraded by the time you receive it. In the past, isinglass required "cutting" in an acid solution for as much as several weeks in order to dissolve it for use. You can now purchase it in powder form, produced by a freeze-dried process, which supposedly dissolves in water in as few as 20 minutes. Just follow the instructions on the packet.

I find I get more consistent results from the following approach. Take a 1-pint jar, add a little water (3–4 ounces, about 100 milliliters), and carefully shred 5 grams isinglass on top of the water, shaking vigorously after each addition. A more sophisticated technique that will avoid the formation of undissolved clumps is to add the isinglass to a dry jar and then add enough straight grain alcohol to wet the powder. Top up the jar with boiled water, add 5 grams tartaric acid, and 1 gram sodium metabisulphite. Seal the jar tightly, shake well, and store in a refrigerator, shaking at frequent intervals over a week or so. Kept cold, these finings will keep for months.

The yeast count should be in the correct range after a week in the primary, followed by a week in the secondary vessel. Rack into the final container, and mix 5–6 ounces of the prepared 1% solution of isinglass with 1 pint of beer. Then add it all to the bulk. Seal the container, and shake vigorously. For best results, the beer should be at around 60 °F (15.6 °C) when fined, and its temperature preferably should rise a few degrees after that point. Primings, if used, should be added at the same time. This technique has consistently given me bright draught beer after around 24 hours, although this result might take a little longer to produce, depending on the yeast you use. Craftbrewers will find it advantageous to do a few tests on a small amount of beer in order to determine the required volume of finings.

You can get more complicated than this and use auxiliary finings. These are usually acidified silicates, or polysaccharide gums, such as carrageenan and gum arabic, or blends of both. These will also remove proteins as well as yeast, thereby leading to better beer colloidal stability.[5] Auxiliary finings are not used on their own. Rather, they are added just prior to fining with isinglass; they will reduce the amount of isinglass required. I have not found them necessary, but craftbrewers might want to explore their use, since they will give the beer better resistance to chill haze formation.

Priming and Carbonation

The purpose of priming is simply to give the finished beer a suitable amount of dissolved carbon dioxide. However, before you ask how much priming you need, you must decide how much carbonation you want in the beer. And before that comes the determination of at what temperature you will serve the beer.

As I mentioned previously, the best temperature is 52–55 °F (11–13 °C). This is the traditional temperature for English draught beer and is the range in which the flavors are best perceived. Colder temperatures tend to dampen the fruity ale character and lessen the impact of hop bitterness. If you prefer the American approach of drinking your beer colder than that, I recommend that you go no lower than about 45 °F (7 °C). Anything less than that, and there is little point in going to great lengths to choose expensive yeasts and complicated hop and grain bills. You are just not going to taste any of the complexities that you have labored to put into the beer.

For reasons that I have never understood, carbon dioxide levels are always measured in volumes of CO_2; a volume is measured at 0 °C and 760 millimeters of mercury pressure. English draught bitter should be served at 1.0–1.5 volumes, preferably toward the lower end of this range. American pale and amber ales and IPAs tend to be served at higher carbonation levels, 2.0–2.5 volumes. This is all really a question of taste, and in that area, there can be no absolutes. But I find that at 2.0 volumes, the gassiness of the beer tends to dominate the flavor, masking many of the subtleties of these styles (although the powerful flavor of Cascades can be difficult to quell!). I also find that a high gas content makes the drink much more filling, so it is difficult for me to drink anything more than one or two pints in a session.

Once you have decided on serving temperature and gas content, how do you get the CO_2 into the beer? For the professional, and for the amateur with a keg set-up, this is fairly straightforward. You simply apply enough pressure to the vessel to achieve the desired level of carbonation. There are published tables that provide the required pressure amounts, in terms of both temperature and carbon dioxide volumes.[6] Note that none of these tables shows as low as 1 volume of CO_2, which requires less than 5 pounds per square inch of applied pressure.

Simply applying a pressure to the headspace above the beer will not readily achieve the carbonation levels you want. This is because carbon dioxide dissolves slowly in beer. Homebrewers often find it necessary to rock the keg violently to get the gas to dissolve quickly. Craftbrewers often use a carbonation stone. a device that disperses the gas as very fine bubbles so that it dissolves much faster. Otherwise, it might take days for the beer to come to equilibrium with the applied gas pressure. Clearly, the higher the final content you want, the longer it will take to reach equilibrium—this is yet another argument in favor of low levels of carbonation.

If you are bottling a beer, things are a little more difficult because you do not know just how much gas is already dissolved in the beer before bottling. Assuming that you have fermented your beer at temperatures in the range 60–70 °F (15.6–21.1 °C), you will have around 0.4–0.5 volumes of CO_2 in the beer. You then have to add enough priming sugar to bring it up to the required level. But bear in mind that this assumes that the beer has reached terminal gravity. If it has not, then any residual fermentable sugar will ferment along with the primings, and the beer might be considerably gassier than you intended.

English brewers use the rule of thumb that finishing gravity should be about one-quarter original gravity.

TABLE 10

Priming and Carbonation
(for 5 U.S. gallons)

Required CO_2 Level	Cane Sugar Addition (oz.)[1]	Corn Sugar Addition (oz.)	Volumes CO_2 added	Final Volumes CO_2 in Beer[2]
1.0	2.0	2.5	0.6	1.0–1.1
1.5	3.5	4.4	1.1	1.5–1.6
2.0	5.0	6.3	1.7	2.1–2.2
2.5	6.0	7.5	2.1	2.5–2.6
3.0	7.5	9.4	2.6	3.0–3.1

[1]Rounded up for convenience.
[2]Assumes 0.4–0.5 volumes of CO_2 in beer before priming.

This can vary, depending on mashing temperatures used by you or by your malt extract manufacturer. If the beer has stayed at the same gravity after several days in the secondary, and your fermentation has proceeded in a normal manner, then you usually can safely assume that you have reached final gravity. It is prudent, however, to allow for this if your gravity is above this one-quarter original gravity value. Simply deduct from the recommended amount of priming 1.5 ounces cane sugar (2 ounces corn sugar) for every one point of gravity (1.001, 0.3 °P) above this value.

You might find table 10 helpful in determining the required amount of priming for a given carbonation level.

I have given cane sugar as the main priming agent and equivalent amounts of corn sugar, allowing for the presence of only about 80% dextrose in corn sugar. Cane sugar is much more convenient and readily available and works equally as well as corn sugar. I really see no need to prime with the latter. As usual, priming is best boiled with a little water, cooled, and then added to the bulk of the beer, before bottling. For kegged or cask-conditioned beer, add the priming along with any finings used.

Bottling and Kegging

This section is really aimed at the homebrewer, since the technology of bottling lines is beyond the scope of this book. Craftbrewers in general have tended to move away from bottle-conditioned beers, favoring either filtration and pasteurization or sterile filtration. That has been very much the trend followed by English brewers during most of the twentieth century, and by the 1970s, just one or two bottle-conditioned beers were available. Only one example, Worthington White Shield, had anything remotely approaching national availability. Even then it was not easy to find in a pub, and there was a good chance the barman did not know how to pour it!

However, one offshoot of the craftbrewing revolution in England has been the rediscovery of bottle-conditioned beers by some of the established brewers, as well as by new brewers. Indeed, there are more than 130 such beers listed in a recent CAMRA publication, although only some of those are pale ales.[7] Oddly, this trend is inspired by some of the big supermarket chains that often offer a range of these beers on their shelves. Even the giant brewer Courage was inspired to bring out its Director's Bitter in this form a few years ago. Unfortunately, they did not do a very good job of it, as the yeast did not compact well. Plus, they used clear bottles, and this often led to unpleasant-tasting, light-struck beer. It since has been withdrawn from the market.

Despite this, many improvements have been made in the technology of producing bottle-conditioned pale ales. These include adding auxiliary finings to the fermenter and then using isinglass in the racking back, and sometimes coarse filtration. This is followed by repitching with yeast, adding priming sugars, storing at ambient temperatures for about one week to develop CO_2, and then cooling to 40–45 °F (4.4–7.2 °C) to allow the yeast to sediment. Recommended shelf life might be up to six months, although six weeks is regarded as ideal.[8] Note that Worthington White Shield was for some years filtered and then repitched with a different, better-sedimenting yeast.

Although, as I mentioned earlier, the homebrewer can filter the beer before bottling. I do not recommend this. Conditioning in the bottle is a simple technique and if properly done produces bottled beer at its best. Indeed, it is as close as you can get to cask-conditioned beer for many homebrewers. However, it generally leads to much higher levels of carbonation (up to 2.0–2.5 volumes CO_2) than can be obtained in a cask. One of the big advantages for the homebrewer is the presence of yeast in the bottle, since yeast is a reducing agent and helps to combat the risk of air oxidation on storage.

Of course, the presence of dissolved air in the beer is often a problem for the amateur.[9] One way around this is to use counter-pressure bottling directly from a keg. This permits you to bottle clarified, force-carbonated beer directly, thereby eliminating the need for priming and enabling you to achieve the carbonation level you want. There are a number of such devices available on the market at reasonable prices (see appendix B).

The other problem with counter-pressure bottling is that it requires a kegging system. If you have a kegging system, why would you want to go to the trouble of bottling? For me, the biggest advance in homebrewing techniques is the wide availability of the stainless steel, soda-keg system. These kegs are much simpler to use than bottles, considerably easier to keep clean, and permit good control of carbonation. They even allow you to produce a sediment-free beer by reracking under pressure. Further, they can be stored in a refrigerator, if desired. I have used nothing else since I discovered them. And I should point out that I have tried every type of plastic keg under the sun. Although plastic kegs are cheaper than stainless steel kegs, they are harder to keep clean and they just do not have the life of the soda kegs.

Soda kegs also are more expensive than bottles. A complete, new, soda-keg system, including a CO_2 cylinder and pressure regulator, will cost you $200 or more. You will probably want more than one keg—new 5-gallon kegs cost $80–$100, although you can pick up used ones more cheaply ($20–$25). But soda kegs will last virtually forever, so the amortized cost per brew is really very low. Running costs are quite cheap. I have had few maintenance problems, and spares are readily available from homebrew dealers. You do need to refill the cylinder. This costs me $11 for my 5-pound tank, but the refilled cylinder lasts me six months or more. (However, I operate at lower gas pressures than is normal for American homebrewers.)

Another advantage of soda kegs is that you can obtain them in the smaller 3-gallon size, which I have found an excellent way to store very strong beers that require long maturation. For more details on the mechanics of handling and selecting kegs, see the articles in appendix B.

Kegs also help in controlling air levels in the beer. Carbon dioxide is denser than air, so you can use it to flush out the keg before racking the beer into it. Once the keg is sealed, you can also flush the headspace two or three times with CO_2. Even better, allow the beer to come to equilibrium with the applied pressure, vent the cask through the pressure relief device, and reapply the pressure, and then repeat the operation. If you have left yeast in the beer, the combination of this approach and the reducing powers of the yeast should minimize air oxidation of the beer. You can permit the beer to clarify under its own steam, but this might be slow, depending on the flocculent nature of the yeast. I usually find it advantageous to fine the beer with isinglass, as discussed in this chapter. You can also dry hop the beer in the keg quite easily simply by suspending a muslin bag full of hops in it. You will need to weight it down (you can actually buy suitable weights from suppliers) to prevent it from floating (do not forget to sanitize the weight). Avoid simply throwing in a handful of hop flowers or pellets. This will block the outlet tube, resulting in a possible safety hazard, as well as being very frustrating when you are thirsty!

An argument against the use of kegs is that you have to push the beer through the serving line and tap by carbon dioxide pressure. This might be all right if you are operating at CO_2 levels of 2.0 volumes and above, but it is not so good if you want a less gassy beer. The problem is that you need about 10 pounds per square inch (psi) for serving. If you maintain that level of pressure on the beer constantly, then the beer will equilibrate with the applied pressure and will contain as much as 2.0 volumes CO_2. There is a very simple way around this that I use. When I fill the keg, I set the regulator to around 5 pounds per square inch and let the beer equilibrate over a few days. I draw off a pint or two, set the regulator to 10 pounds per square inch, open the valve, allow the pressures to balance, and then turn off the valve. The valve is opened only when the flow of beer slows while serving, and it remains open just for a few minutes. In that way, the pressure in the keg always remains close to 5 pounds per square inch and the beer is perfect, no gassier than any real ale served from a cask by a beer engine.

This last technique amounts to top-pressure serving (in CAMRA terms), while a constant applied pressure is basically artificial carbonation. Note that when the pressure in the keg is the same, there is no difference in flavor due to artificial carbonation in the presence of yeast, as opposed to priming by secondary fermentation (although CAMRA diehards would prefer the latter). However, the top-pressure technique does permit you to operate at much lower gas levels, similar to those obtained with cask-conditioning, but without the ingress of air. You cannot let in air, as is the custom with real ale, unless the beer is to be consumed in a day or two. If you expect it to last a matter of weeks, you must keep the air out to prevent spoilage.

Finally, kegs permit you to experiment with the newest fad in dispensing beer: the use of mixed gas (nitrogen and carbon dioxide). This has become very trendy in England, especially among the big factory brewers. The technique was pioneered by Guinness and is the secret behind the big, creamy head, formed by very fine bubbles, of the company's stout. It is also what is used in cans of Guinness and the cans of "pub beer" from England, now available in America. The logic behind its use is that nitrogen is much less soluble in beer. Thus, by using mixed gas you can apply a high pressure to the beer, while the level of carbon dioxide dissolved remains low enough for the beer in the glass not to be gassy.[10]

Mixed gases can be used at home, but I do not see that this is something the homebrewer would or should do.[11] It does simplify life a little for the pub operator trying to dispense beer through long lines. But, then, if he operated with a less gassy beer to start with and pumped it mechanically, he would not have the problem in the first place. In fact, I think there is a big disadvantage in serving the pale ale style of beer in this manner. This is because a good deal of the hop bitterness and character is swept up by the big head that is formed and consequently lost to the body of the beer. For a beer that depends to a great extent on these flavor aspects, this can be a disaster. A big creamy head might look good, but it can make the beer beneath it flabby and uninteresting.

Cask Conditioning

I have already described what I mean by cask-conditioned, and what real ale is. To recap, cask conditioning is the process by which the green beer is racked into a cask, primed and fined, and shipped to the pub. In the pub's cellar, it undergoes a secondary fermentation, during which the cask is vented in a controlled manner. Once the secondary fermentation has subsided, the beer is allowed to sit for a few days. It then is served directly from the cask by mechanical means (a beer engine or an electric pump). It must not be pushed from the cask by carbon dioxide. As the beer is drawn off, air is allowed into the cask, so the cask must be emptied within a couple of days or so; otherwise, the beer will spoil. The priming level is controlled to give a relatively low gas content of around 1 volume CO_2.

In American usage, the terms *keg* and *cask* are interchangeable. All draught containers tend to be called kegs in America, but in England a keg is most definitely not a cask. A keg is designed for serving bright beer under carbon dioxide pressure and has only one central entry point, called a spear. The gas is forced down the spear, and beer is driven up it to the point of dispense. You cannot draw beer from a keg by means of a tap, and the beer will always be gassy because it is driven by gas.

A cask has the traditional rounded barrel shape, with an arched body flanked by flat ends, or heads. One of the heads has a hole at the bottom suited to take a tap; it is usually fitted with a brass bushing called a keystone. In the middle of the arched side, in a plane passing vertically through the keystone, is a much larger hole, about two inches in diameter, called the shive hole. This is usually fitted with a brass collar. At the brewery, both the shive hole and the keystone are fitted with wooden plugs, called shives. The keystone shive is half cut out so that a metal or wooden tap can be banged through it. The residue of the shive remains as a seal around the tap. The tap itself might be constructed to take a cone of fine metal gauze inside its body so as to prevent hop flowers (used for dry hopping) from clogging the dispense lines.

On arrival in the cellar, the cask is put on stillage—that is, resting on its curved side so that the heads are vertical and the shive hole is at the top. Stillage can be simply a couple of shaped blocks, a set of X-shaped legs connected by struts (with the cask sitting on the top half of the X), or any similar arrangement to hold the cask steady and slightly tilted towards the tap. The shive is partly drilled (0.25 inch or so in diameter). After the cask is stillaged, this hole is knocked through completely, and a wooden spile is fitted. A spile is a conical peg; it comes in two forms. The first is porous and made from bamboo; the second is nonporous hard wood. When the shive is drilled out, a porous spile is first inserted into the hole. It is placed firmly in position but not hammered home so that it can easily be removed by hand. In the early stages of the secondary fermentation, some foaming through the spile will occur and must be carefully and frequently wiped away. Once the beer is properly conditioned and foaming ceases, the porous spile is replaced by a hard spile so that no more gas can escape. The exact timing of this is crucial to the proper serving of real ale; it is something that can be learned only by experience. (However, it usually is from 36 to 48 hours at normal cellar temperatures.)

The hard spile is kept in place until the beer is ready to serve. The tap, if not already in place, is hammered home and connected to the lines. The hard spile then is removed, and the beer is dispensed. In rare cases, the dispense might be done by gravity. More often, it is pulled off by a beer engine or an electric pump. At the end of each serving session, the hard spile should be replaced so that the beer does not lose condition.

This is the traditional approach to preparing real, cask-conditioned ale. Its devotees (of whom I am one) will tell you that the resulting beer is bitter at its best, with a soft, fruity flavor unmatched by beer dispensed by any other method. There is some disagreement in England as to whether the beer should be served with a head. In the South, it is pulled from the hand pump so as to have a minimal head. In the North, drinkers like the little device on the spout, a restricted orifice called a sparkler, that is screwed home tightly so that an inch or so of close-bubbled head is formed. Some drinkers even argue that the beer is formulated and brewed according to whether it will have a head and that one brewed to have no head will be spoiled by pulling it out of a tight sparkler.[12] Appendix B lists some excellent resources on producing real ale, whether at home or as a professional brewer.

It takes a great deal of care, skill, and knowledge to maintain cask beer at its best. Several English brewers have in the past operated various schemes to train and reward publicans who keep their beer well. In 1998, a number of national and regional brewers were recruited to a new scheme, called Cask Marque. In the first stages, regular visits will be made to participating pubs and plaques awarded to those whose beers consistently pass taste tests. Periodic inspections will be done and plaques withdrawn from those whose beer falls in quality.[13] It remains to be seen how well this scheme works. However, the fact that it is seen as needed indicates how difficult it is to keep real ale in good condition. Poorly trained staff, failure to control cellar temperature properly, and mis-judgment of turnover rates—all result in poor-quality ale that is cloudy, flat, or even downright vinegary! This makes real ale a rarity in America, where brewpub staffs have no idea how to handle it and only a few brewers are willing to take the risk with it. Indeed, I have run across quite a few brewpubs that offer "cask-conditioned beer" that actually is nothing of the sort. It is simply kegged, clarified beer (sometimes even lightly filtered) that has undergone no sort of secondary fermentation in cask and is sometimes kept under a blanket of nitrogen.

Offering the genuine article can be done, and a few intrepid brewers do so. (See appendix B for some useful articles on the subject.) They might, however, have to make some changes in the brewing process to suit American conditions. Pike Place, for example, conditions the beer in cask at the brewery (without fining, since fining does not suit their yeast). It then draws off the sediment immediately before delivery, so the beer can be served right away in the bar or pub.[14] Other breweries, such as Hales Ales of Seattle, also offer a bright, racked "real ale," although it certainly does not deserve that designation if dispensed with carbon dioxide.

Attempts have been made to modify the traditional process in England, especially for pubs where the beer might have a low turnover rate and will therefore go flat and spoil. The most important modification is the so-called "cask breather." Basically, the cask breather permits the ingress of carbon dioxide or nitrogen, at atmospheric pressure, instead of air, as the beer is drawn off. It carries a relief valve to prevent any buildup of pressure so that the beer does not become gassier during its serving life and does not oxidize due to the presence of air.[15] It is used by a number of well-respected traditional and regional brewers, who swear that it is the only way to handle slow-moving casks. CAMRA has officially proscribed its use for real ale, but the argument between its members about this has been long and heated. The cask breather does not let in air, and some people think that the effects of air might actually be beneficial over the short life of a cask (long-term effects of air are agreed to be bad). Evidence for this is anecdotal, but it seems unlikely that air really affects flavor in this way.

Casks

Today, most English (and American) brewers use stainless steel casks. Of course, to be really traditional you would use a wooden cask. A limited number of English brewers still do that, and a few—Young's and Sam Smith among them—still have their own coopers to make and repair the wooden casks. Aficionados consider this to be the only way to serve real ale. Wooden casks give better control over temperature than do steel casks. They also are capable of adding something extra to the beer's flavor. This flavor comes not so much from the wood itself, but from various microflora that dwell in it.

The use of coopered casks goes back centuries and is based on sound engineering principles. The staves of the casks are tapered from end to end on all four sides so that the resultant arch shape of the cask is reinforced in both the vertical and horizontal planes. The staves are forced into tight contact with one another by means of metal hoops. Today, wooden casks are often partially assembled by machine methods, although there are still a number of traditional coopers left who assemble them entirely by hand (most of these are in the Scotch whisky industry, unfortunately for brewers). Their occupation still requires a four-year apprenticeship and membership in a guild that goes back to the early fourteenth century in England. In the hand coopering of a cask, only the length of the staves and the diameter of the head are actually measured. All other cutting and shaving is estimated by sight and done by hand. In today's machine era, it is a delight to watch a cooper at work. I recommend it, if you ever get the chance.

The old and the new—a traditional English coopered wooden cask and a modern version in stainless steel.

Originally, the cask was made of English oak, but this wood is now virtually a vanished commodity. Polish oak now seems to be the favored raw material, although both German and Russian oak are also suitable. According to the cooper who made my casks, these oaks are relatively nonporous when properly cut—this is what helps to make them so watertight. They also have virtually no "oaking" effect on the beer's flavor, and that has certainly been my experience with my own casks. Apparently, English coopers were forced to use American oak during World War II and found it quite unsuitable. American oak resins leached out into the beer, giving it an undesirable flavor, and the only solution was to line the casks with pitch. If you are going to do that, you might just as well use a steel cask, which is easier to handle.

Effect of Wood on Flavor

The role of oak *flavor* in beer is mysterious. It is unknown whether the casks used in the Burton Unions added an oak flavor to the original pale ales. Marston's is the only English brewer to still use unions. It reports a somewhat different initial flavor when the unions are freshly scraped out, as happens every three years or so.[16] But my own experience brewing in and drinking beers from oak casks suggests that the typical oaky character so often seen in the ubiquitous Chardonnays is not a part of pale ale flavor. But then there is Ballantine's IPA and its renowned American oak flavor. However, as I discussed in chapter 1, this probably came from maturing in wooden tanks, rather than from the casks used to transport the beer.

Fermenting and maturing in wood is rare these days and is usually reserved for fairly strong beers that need lengthy maturation. However, Gale's of Hampshire reportedly uses fermenters made of a type of pine imported from New Zealand and prefers the flavor of beer made in these to that produced in stainless steel vessels.[17] I am quite familiar with Gale's fine beers, which do have a malty, complex character. But I cannot remember ever detecting any taste notes that I could assign to pine. The Firestone Walker Brewing Company in California is also said to use American oak casks in a Union-type system that gives the beer a distinctive oaky character.[18]

In his article "Beer from the Wood," Jason Dunson-Todd recommends the use of oak, and the American variety in particular. He suggests that all pale ales, and even medium-gravity bitters, would nicely pick up oak flavors.[19] The beer will pick up some tannins, which could cause harsh flavors in a low-gravity beer. This might not be a problem, however, since by definition such beers are not matured for long periods of time. And of course, there are all of the other oaky flavors, such as vanillins, which are so prominent in many modern Chardonnays. While this approach would certainly add some complexity to the beer, it also would take the beer out of the classic pale ale style. Still, that is no reason not to do it. I have said elsewhere that classic definitions should not be regarded as restrictive. If you are interested in trying it, go ahead, push back the frontiers.

Another approach, tried in America, is to add oak chips to the maturing beer. This might have been inspired by Budweiser's much publicized use of beechwood chips for aging. In fact, these confer no flavor at all. Using them is simply a way of providing a large surface area to help pick up yeast and clarify the beer. Pike Place reportedly used this technique at one time, aging an IPA on French oak chips, but they have now discontinued this beer because of a lack of interest from their customers.[20] If you want to try aging on wood chips, go ahead, although you might find sanitation a problem. Boiling the chips is likely to remove a lot of the flavoring substances from the oak, and less stringent sanitation methods might leave infecting bacteria in the wood pores. But, as I said previously, it might add some extra complexity, so try it by all means!

Wood versus Stainless Steel

I do have some problems with wooden casks, especially for the homebrewer who is likely to have them out of use for significant periods of time. First, a cask should not be allowed to dry out, as its staves will shrink and it will no longer be watertight. You have to keep it filled with water. But you can accomplish this only very gradually because it takes some time for the staves to soak up the water and expand, thereby becoming watertight. I had a bad experience doing this when I moved to America from England, bringing with me a couple of casks. It took nearly two months of soaking before they finally ceased to leak!

A second problem with wooden casks is the difficulty of cleaning one that might have all sorts of unpleasant contamination lodged in the wood. Even when in use, casks can become contaminated, particularly if they are left sitting around still containing some beer dregs. Cleaning them out thoroughly is very difficult unless you have access to live steam. You can give them a short soak in dilute bleach solution, but they will need several soakings and rinses after such treatment. And I can tell you that heaving about even a 5-gallon cask when full of water is quite an exercise.

For these reasons, you are probably better off getting new casks, or least remade casks. I really recommend that if you want to brew real ale at home, you stick with stainless steel casks. These will last a very long time, do not leak, and are much easier to clean than wooden casks. Note, however, that their shape and narrow entry orifices make cleaning them more difficult than is the case with the soda kegs. In fact, you can use a soda keg to dispense true real ale. [21] Lay the keg horizontally, with the gas inlet on the bottom and the long outlet tube at the top. Then dispense the beer through the "in" valve, while admitting air through the "out" valve, which has been fitted with a quick disconnect hose-barb attachment. There is no reason why this should not work well, but I must admit I have not tried it, largely because the beer must all be consumed in a day or two or oxidation will result.

A stainless steel soda keg, ready for dispensing one of my IPAs, alongside a vertical cask designed for real ale storage. Who wants to wash bottles?

Casks can be fairly expensive—$100 and up for American oak or American stainless steel casks.[22] Imported casks, whether wooden or metal, are obviously more expensive. And note that English casks come in some odd sizes. Smallest (and rarest in America) is the *pin*, which contains 4.5 imperial gallons (about 5.5 U.S. gallons). Next is the *firkin*, at 9 imperial gallons (10.5 U.S. gallons), followed by the 18-imperial-gallon *kilderkin* and the 36-imperial-gallon barrel. Incidentally, apart from the barrel, the names of the other three are Dutch in origin, reflecting the fact that the first beer brewers (as opposed to ale brewers) in England were from the Netherlands. Having said all that, I have just bought a stainless steel pin for $85. Unlike more traditional casks, this one is straight-sided, with the keystone at the bottom and the shive hole in the top. I have not tried it yet, but there is no reason why it should not work as well as the traditional barrel shape. And it will, of course, need no stillage.

In addition to the casks, you will need a variety of other equipment. These include

- shives,
- spiles,
- taps (stainless steel is best, but brass is the most common),
- a wooden mallet (for banging home shives and taps), and
- a shive extractor.

If you are going to take the "authentic" English approach and connect your cask to a beer engine, you also will need suitable tubing and, of course, a beer engine. The engine will probably set you back another $250 to $300 or so. An alternative is to build one yourself, as described by Sal Emma in his article, "Build a Beer Engine."[23]

Dispensing through a Beer Engine

Beer engines have existed in England since early in the nineteenth century. They are not essential to the serving of real ale, but do add a nice touch and give you much better control over head formation than does gravity dispense. Although called a beer engine, it is more properly a hand pump, in that it operates entirely manually. It consists of a cylinder, which is usually 0.5 imperial pint in volume and fitted with a plunger. As you pull on the handle, the plunger pulls the beer up to the spout and into the glass. As the handle is returned to the vertical, a flap valve in the plunger opens and the cylinder refills with beer. In England, the presence of a hand pump on the bar can imply that the pub is selling real ale. While this is often true, it is also possible to use one to dispense from a cask that carries a top-pressure of carbon dioxide and does not permit the entry of air into the cask.

In modern times, electric pumps were introduced. These offer an advantage over hand pumps in that they can meter in exact quantities. They are quite widely used, but many brewers and publicans still prefer the hand pump, perhaps as much for its aesthetic qualities as for its practicality.

Today, there are two types of hand pumps, distinguished by the shape of the delivery spout, as I mentioned earlier in this chapter. The standard one is quite short, often just a straight horizontal tube with a short, wide tap at one end. This is the type that has been used for dispensing beers in the south of England for as long as I have been drinking beer. The second type has a long arching tube, or swan neck, ending in a fairly narrow orifice. This is a somewhat newer design and has become accepted as the standard for Northern beers.

A pair of antique handpumps, or beer engines, along with a rear view of the bar in my home brewery.

Both types can be fitted with a sparkler, which is adjustable and can be screwed up or down to increase or decrease its effect. The turbulence caused by forcing the beer through the restricted orifices of the sparkler generates foaming by the evolution of carbon dioxide and by air pickup. A tight sparkler gives the beer a very thick, dense head, while a loose one gives it a much fluffier, smaller head. Without the sparkler, as used to be common, the beer is often served with virtually no head at all (depending on its condition).

Both types of hand pumps have their devotees in England, but in recent years the swan neck types have spread all over the country, and beer with a big head has become common, even in the South. Many English drinkers feel that this is wrong and that the choice of nozzle should depend on the beer, rather than the other way round. As always, it is an issue that is clouded by ancient North-South enmity that often gets in the way of rational judgment. The argument is that because many hop bittering and aroma components have significant surface activity, they will be concentrated in the big head of a beer pulled from a swan neck. This will leave the body of the beer emasculated and uninteresting. This is certainly true if the head is overdone. However, it is still possible with a swan neck to produce a beer with a modest head that does not suffer from this effect. Of course, others say that a tight head actually leads to an emphasis on the hop aromatic character. It probably would not hurt an American pale ale or IPA to be pulled off in this way because of their characteristic high hop character.

I feel that this is really a personal choice; you have to decide for yourself on the type of hand pump to use. If you are not sure, then go for the swan neck, as I have done— a new clamp-on type costs me $325. Experiment with the sparkler position or even leave it off, using the same beer. Once you have found what works for you, leave it that way for future brews. Craftbrewers might have the choice made for them by their customers. It might well be worth educating them as to which you think is best for your type of beer. If time permits, you would be well advised to demonstrate your desired approach to them.

I have included in appendix B a list of sources that include names of suppliers of casks, kegs, hand pumps, and accessories. I have not checked out all of these suppliers; some might deal only on a wholesale basis. Homebrewers might have to work through the lists to find someone prepared to supply retail (although I found one straightaway when I recently bought a pin and hand pump from an East Coast supplier).

Serving Pale Ale

Finally, what are you going to dispense the beer into? A glass, naturally, but what sort of glass? In my opinion, neither American nor English brewers pay enough attention to their glasses for bitters and pale ales. The so-called "shaker pint" used by many American craftbreweries and brewpubs is heavy and unattractive and does little to enhance the enjoyment of drinking. When I first started going to pubs in England, this style of glass was used only in public bars, where cheapness was a major consideration. The up-market saloon and private bars would use something a little better, usually the dimpled mug. This is not so bad, but it is a little heavy and clumsy and not exactly stylish. Some of the newer thin straight glasses, or sleeves, used in England are an improvement. But surely modern design techniques could come up with something much better and more interesting. Belgian brewers in particular are fastidious about ensuring that their beer is served from a suitable and attractive, usually badged, glass, so why do we not also?

I am something of a glass fanatic. I have a collection of around 200 different styles from all over the world, but particularly from England and America. Surprisingly few of them are all that interesting in terms of design—many are more important to me as nostalgic reminders of beers I have drunk. So this is a plea to brewers everywhere: Pale ale is one of the most important beer styles in the world, so why can we not have glasses that match that importance?

CHAPTER 5

Pale Ale
Recipes

The subject of this chapter should be self-explanatory from the title, but there are a few points to make before I list the actual recipes.

Each recipe has three versions, one based on a 1-barrel scale and two on 5-gallon volumes. One of the latter two is a full-mash brew, while the other is from malt extract. All of the recipes are intended to result in similar beers, but the beers are unlikely to be identical, due to brewing differences in all three. All are tested, but I had to make assumptions about grain extraction rates, boil times, and hop utilization rates. These are listed next. If your parameters differ from those listed, you will need to adjust hopping rates and grain amounts. Remember that using different quantities of grain will alter the color of the beer, although the values given in the recipes are only estimates and you might get more or less color than I have indicated, depending on malt source and the amount of caramelization obtained in the copper.

Malt Extract
- Plain, unhopped malt extract only
- Water treatment for flavor only
- Boil time of only 45 minutes
- Hop utilization of 20% for pellets and 18% for hop flowers for a full boil (less if doing only a partial boil), with hops added at the start of boil
- Crystal and roasted grain malts crushed and steeped in hot (not boiling) water, with the liquor separated from the grain before boiling

5-Gallon Grain Mash
- 1.030 (7.6 °P) per pound per gallon for pale malt
- 1.025 (6.3 °P) per pound per gallon for crystal malts
- Water treatment indicates desired values after treatment
- Boil time of 90 minutes

- Hop utilization of 25% for flowers and 28% for pellets (no allowance is made for wort gravity)

1-Barrel Grain Mash
- 1.035 (8.8 °P) per pound per gallon for pale malt
- 1.025 (6.3 °P) per pound per gallon for crystal malts
- Water treatment indicates desired values after treatment
- Boil time of 90 minutes
- Hop utilization of 30% for flowers and 33% for pellets (no allowance is made for wort gravity)
- Ability to use different yeast strains (in practice, craftbrewers might wish to stay with only one strain)
- Specialty malts and aroma hops scaled up from the 5-gallon brew—adjustments possible to suit individual brew house performance

All fermentations should be carried out at 60–70 °F (15.6–21.1 °C), and priming and preferred method of dispense are as indicated in the recipes. For draft beers, fining with isinglass is optional. Serving temperatures are optional, but I would not drink any of these beers at anything other than 52–55 °F (11–16 °C), given the choice.

The extract beers, as presented, use extract only as the base malts. This can sometimes result in a thin-tasting beer, which can be improved by the partial mashing technique. Follow these steps:

1. Replace 1 pound extract with 2 pounds pale malt.
2. Mash this with 1–2 quarts water at around 150 °F (65.5 °C).
3. Strain off the liquor, and rinse the mash with hot water.
4. Add the collected runnings to the kettle.

For the mash beers, use 1–2 quarts of water per pound of malt in the mash. Sparge with water at around 170 °F (77 °C), using enough to compensate for evaporative loss during boiling. Your final brew length will be as indicated in the recipe.

All of these recipes should be regarded as flexible. You do not have to copy them directly and should feel free to experiment with different ingredients. This is particularly true of the hop varieties and of late-hopping schedules. One of the great advances on the small brewing scene, particularly for homebrewers, is the wide choice of hops now available. So go to it. Make the most of this diversity, and put your own spin on these recipes. Perhaps you can create yet another substyle of pale ale!

Ordinary Bitters

Quarter Session Bitter

Malt	Extract 5 Gal.	All-Grain 5 Gal.	All-Grain 1 Bbl.
Pale malt syrup	4.0 lb. (1.82 kg) (78.8%)	—	—
Pale dry malt extract	0.7 lb. (318 g) (13.8%)	—	—
140 °L crystal malt	0.375 lb. (170 g) (7.4%)	0.375 lb. (170 g) (6%)	2.4 lb. (1.09 kg) (6.9%)
British two-rowed pale malt	—	5.6 lb. (2.54 kg) (90%)	30.4 lb. (13.8 kg) (88%)
Wheat malt	—	0.25 lb. (114 g) (4%)	1.75 lb. (795 g) (5.1%)
Beer color (°SRM)	14	14	14

Hops	Extract 5 Gal.	All-Grain 5 Gal.	All-Grain 1 Bbl.
Bittering Hops			
WGV hop flowers (4.9% AA)	2.5 oz. (71 g)	1.8 oz. (51 g)	9.6 oz. (272 g)
HBU	12.3	8.8	—
IBU	33	33	33
Aroma Hops			
WGV hop flowers (end of boil)	0.5 oz. (14 g)	0.5 oz. (14 g)	3.2 oz. (91 g)

Specifications

Original gravity:	1.037 (9.3 °P)
Final gravity:	1.007–1.009 (1.8–2.3 °P) for extract 5 gal.
	1.008–1.010 (2.1–2.6 °P) for all-grain 5 gal. and 1 bbl.
Water treatment:	Calcium 50–100 ppm; sulfate 100–200 ppm; chloride 20 ppm
Mash temperature:	152–154 °F (66.7–67.8 °C)
Yeast:	Wyeast 1028 London Ale
Alcohol v/v:	3.7% approximately
Serve:	Draught only
Priming:	2–3 oz. (56–85 g) cane sugar
CO_2 v/v:	1.0–1.5

Use of dark crystal malt gives this beer a reddish tint and a nutty flavor. Whitbread Goldings varieties add a nice, slightly lemony, spicy flavor and a little complexity to what is really a simple session beer.

Best Bitters

Double Pride Bitter

Malt	Extract 5 Gal.	All-Grain 5 Gal.	All-Grain 1 Bbl.
Pale malt syrup	5.0 lb. (2.27 kg) (83.2%)	—	—
Pale dry malt extract	0.7 lb. (318 g) (11.6%)	—	—
60 °L crystal malt	5.0 oz. (142 g) (5.2%)	5.0 oz. (142 g) (4.2%)	2.0 lb. (908 g) (4.9%)
British two-rowed pale malt	—	7.1 lb. (3.2 kg) (95.8%)	38.8 lb. (17.6 kg) (95.1%)
Beer color (°SRM)	8.0	8.0	8.0

Hops	Extract 5 Gal.	All-Grain 5 Gal.	All-Grain 1 Bbl.
Bittering Hops			
WGV hop flowers (4.9% AA)	2.25 oz. (64 g)	1.6 oz. (45 g)	8.7 oz. (247 g)
HBU	11.0	7.8	—
IBU	30	30	30
Aroma Hops			
WGV hop flowers (20 min.)	0.5 oz. (14 g)	0.5 oz. (14 g)	3.0 oz. (85 g)
Goldings (end of boil)	0.5 oz. (14 g)	0.5 oz. (14 g)	3.0 oz. (85 g)

Specifications

Original gravity:	1.044 (11 °P)
Final gravity:	1.008–1.011 (2.1–2.6 °P) for extract 5 gal.
	1.009–1.011 (2.3–2.8 °P) for all-grain 5 gal. and 1 bbl.
Water treatment:	Calcium 50–100 ppm; sulfate 100–200 ppm; chloride 20 ppm
Mash temperature:	152 °F (66.7 °C)
Yeast:	Wyeast 1028 London Ale
Alcohol v/v:	4.5% approximately
Serve:	Draught only
Priming:	2.2–3.2 oz. (62–91 g) cane sugar
CO_2 v/v:	1.2–1.7

This beer is quite malty, although it is still very bitter and hoppy, with more late hopping than in previous recipes. It has a simple malt bill, so the beer is quite pale but still has some caramel undertones. The name is a play on Fuller's London Pride and the fact that a London soccer team, Arsenal, completed the "double" of both English Premier League Championship and the Football Association Cup in the 1997–1998 season.

I Could've Been a Contender Bitter

Malt	Extract 5 Gal.	All-Grain 5 Gal.	All-Grain 1 Bbl.
Pale malt syrup	6.0 lb. (2.72 kg) (88.1%)	—	—
Pale dry malt extract	6.0 oz. (170 g) (5.5%)	—	—
British two-rowed pale malt	—	7.6 lb. (3.45 kg) (94.6%)	42.0 lb. (19.1 kg) (93.7%)
80 °L crystal malt	6.0 oz. (170 g) (5.5%)	6.0 oz. (170 g) (4.7%)	2.4 lb. (1.1 kg) (5.4%)
Black malt	1.0 oz. (28 g) (0.9%)	1.0 oz. (28 g) (0.8%)	0.4 lb. (182 g) (0.9%)
Beer color (°SRM)	17	17	16

Hops	Extract 5 Gal.	All-Grain 5 Gal.	All-Grain 1 Bbl.
Bittering Hops			
Challenger hop flowers (8.6% AA)	1.7 oz. (48 g)	1.2 oz. (34 g)	6.6 oz. (187 g)
HBU	14.6	10.3	—
IBU	40	40	40
Aroma Hop			
Challenger hop flowers (end of boil)	1.0 oz. (28 g)	1.0 oz. (28 g)	5.0 oz. (142 g)

Specifications

Original gravity:	1.048 (11.9 °P)
Final gravity:	1.010–1.012 (2.6–3.1 °P)
Water treatment:	Calcium 50–100 ppm; sulfate 100–200 ppm; chloride 20 ppm
Mash temperature:	152 °F (66.7 °C)
Yeast:	Ringwood
Alcohol v/v:	4.9% approximately
Serve:	Draught only
Priming:	3.0 oz. (85 g) cane sugar
CO_2 v/v:	1.5

Pale Ale

This is a fruity "premium" bitter, with some deep red tints from black malt and plenty of hop character and bitterness. This is a beer to drink a little more reflectively than one might session brews. Full flavor permits carbonation toward the high end of the range for draught beers. The name comes from the liberal use of Challenger hops, what you might call a "pun"-ch!

Special Bitters

Bull's Eye Bitter

Malt	Extract 5 Gal.	All-Grain 5 Gal.	All-Grain 1 Bbl.
Pale malt syrup	6.0 lb. (2.72 kg) (80.0%)	—	—
Pale dry malt extract	1.0 lb. (454 g) (13.3%)	—	—
British two-rowed pale malt	—	8.75 lb. (3.97 kg) (94.6%)	48.0 lb. (21.8 kg) (93.8%)
120 °L crystal malt	0.5 lb. (227 g) (6.7%)	0.5 lb. (227 g) (5.4%)	3.2 lb. (1.45 kg) (6.3%)
Beer color (°SRM)	17	17	17

Hops	Extract 5 Gal.	All-Grain 5 Gal.	All-Grain 1 Bbl.
Bittering Hops			
Target hop pellets (11.1% AA)	1.1 oz. (31 g)	0.8 oz (23 g)	4.4 oz. (125 g)
HBU	12.2	8.9	—
IBU	34	34	36
Aroma Hops			
Saaz hop flowers (end of boil)	0.5 oz. (14 g)	0.5 oz. (14 g)	3.0 oz. (85 g)

Specifications

Original gravity:	1.055 (13.6 °P)
Final gravity:	1.012–1.014 (3.1–3.6 °P)
Water treatment:	Calcium 50–100 ppm; sulfate 100–200 ppm; chloride 20 ppm
Mash temperature:	152 °F (66.7 °C)
Yeast:	Brewlab 1110 Thames Valley 3
Alcohol v/v:	5.6% approximately
Serve:	Draught or bottle
Priming:	3.0–3.5 oz. (85–100 g) cane sugar
CO_2 v/v:	1.5 for draught; 1.5–2.0 for bottle

Pale Ale

This is a darkish beer, more of an amber than a red color. It should have a fair amount of esters and a very clean bitterness from the Target, with just a hint of spice from the Saaz aroma hops. It is quite full bodied, with a lot of caramel undertones. The name comes from the use of Target hops.

English Pale Ales

White Flag Pale Ale

Malt	Extract 5 Gal.	All-Grain 5 Gal.	All-Grain 1 Bbl.
Pale malt syrup	6.0 lb. (2.72 kg) (80.0%)	—	—
Pale dry malt extract	1.0 lb. (454 g) (13.3%)	—	—
English Maris Otter two-rowed pale malt	—	8.75 lb. (3.97 kg) (94.6%)	48.0 lb. (21.8 kg) (93.8%)
20 °L crystal malt	0.5 lb. (227 g) (6.7%)	0.5 lb. (227 g) (5.4%)	3.2 lb. (1.45 kg) (6.2%)
Beer color (°SRM)	7	7	7

Hops	Extract 5 Gal.	All-Grain 5 Gal.	All-Grain 1 Bbl.
Bittering Hops			
Goldings hop flowers (7.8% AA)	1.9 oz. (54 g)	1.4 oz. (40 g)	7.3 oz. (207 g)
HBU	14.8	10.9	—
IBU	40	41	40
Aroma Hops			
Goldings hop flowers (end of boil)	1.0 oz. (28 g)	1.0 oz. (28 g)	60.0 oz. (170 g)

Specifications

Original gravity:	1.055 (13.6 °P)
Final gravity:	1.012–1.014 (3.1–3.6 °P)
Water treatment:	Calcium 100–150 ppm; sulfate 200–300 ppm; chloride 30 ppm
Mash temperature:	154 °F (68 °C)
Yeast:	Williams's Y21 Burton Ale
Alcohol v/v:	5.6% approximately
Serve:	In bottle (preferably bottle-conditioned)
Priming:	3.5–5.0 oz. (100–140 g) cane sugar
CO_2 v/v:	1.5–2.0

Pale Ale

This is a very distinctive pale ale. It has a high level of clean bitterness that is balanced by the nuttiness from the crystal malt and a chewy, grainy character from the yeast, as well as some citric, aromatic notes from the late-hopped Goldings. It is something along the line of Worthington White Shield (although not a direct copy). The name reflects Bass's surrender of its great tradition when it recently ceased to brew this ale.

English IPAs

Back to the Fuchsia IPA

Malt	Extract 5 Gal.	All-Grain 5 Gal.	All-Grain 1 Bbl.
Pale malt syrup	6.0 lb. (2.72 kg) (74.1%)	—	—
Pale dry malt extract	1.6 lb. (726 g) (19.8%)	—	—
English Maris Otter two-rowed pale malt	—	9.5 lb. (4.3 kg) (95.0%)	52.6 lb. (23.9 kg) (94.3%)
40 °L crystal malt	0.5 lb. (227 g) (6.2%)	0.5 lb. (227 g) (5.0%)	3.2 lb. (1.45 kg) (5.7%)
Beer color (°SRM)	10	10	9

Hops	Extract 5 Gal.	All-Grain 5 Gal.	All-Grain 1 Bbl.
Bittering Hops			
Phoenix hop flowers (10.9% AA)	1.5 oz. (43 g)	1.1 oz. (31 g)	5.9 oz. (168 g)
HBU	16.4	12	—
IBU	44	45	45
Aroma Hops			
Phoenix hop flowers (end of boil)	1.0 oz. (28 g)	1.0 oz. (28 g)	6.0 oz. (170 g)

Specifications

Original gravity:	1.060 (14.7 °P)
Final gravity:	1.013–1.016 (3.3–4.1 °P)
Water treatment:	Calcium 100–150 ppm; sulfate 200–300 ppm; chloride 30 ppm
Mash temperature:	152 °F (66.7 °C)
Yeast:	Williams's Y21 Burton Ale
Alcohol v/v:	6.0% approximately
Serve:	Draught or bottle
Priming:	3.0–5.0 oz. (57–140 g) cane sugar
CO_2 v/v:	1.5 for draught; 2.0 for bottle

Pale Ale

This is a more traditional IPA, except for the hop variety used. It has a small amount of pale crystal malt to add a little more body and background caramel and is quite high in bitterness to balance the strength. It should be sipped slowly while sitting in a deck chair watching somebody else weed the flowerbeds. That idea and the use of a new hop variety are the sources of the name.

Original IPA

Malt	Extract 5 Gal.	All-Grain 5 Gal.	All-Grain 1 Bbl.
Pale malt syrup	5.0 lb. (2.3 kg) (56.8%)	—	—
Pale dry malt extract	3.8 lb. (1.73 kg) (43.2%)	—	—
English Maris Otter two-rowed pale malt	—	11.7 lb. (5.31 kg) (100%)	64 lb. (29.1 kg) (100%)
Beer color (°SRM)	8	7	6

Hops	Extract 5 Gal.	All-Grain 5 Gal.	All-Grain 1 Bbl.
Bittering Hops			
Goldings hop flowers (7.8% AA)	6.5 oz. (185 g)	4.7 oz. (134 g)	25.0 oz. (710 g)
HBU	50.7	36.7	—
IBU	About 120	About 120	About 120
Aroma Hops			
Goldings hop flowers (end of boil)	10.0 oz. (28 g)	1.0 oz. (28 g)	6.0 oz. (170 g)

Specifications

Original gravity:	1.070 (17.1 °P)
Final gravity:	1.015–1.017 (3.8–4.3 °P)
Water treatment:	Calcium 150–200 ppm; sulfate 300–400 ppm; chloride 30 ppm
Mash temperature:	153 °F (67.2 °C)
Yeast:	Ringwood
Alcohol v/v:	6.8% approximately
Serve:	Bottle
Priming:	0.5 oz. (14 g) cane sugar
CO₂ v/v:	2.0

1.068 @ 70° (handwritten)

Pale Ale

This is the brew referred to in chapter 1, and as I said there, it is my adaptation of a recipe from the Durden Park Beer Circle. This one differs slightly from the recipe given in chapter 1 for the 5-gallon mash brew, which reflects the difference in extract I normally get, as compared with that used for the Durden Park recipes. Also, the IBU figure quoted is very approximate, as I have never measured it and I do not know what utilization you will get at such very high hop rates. The low priming rates reflect the fact that this beer should be matured in bottle for at least six months.

Unquestionably, the hop bitterness dominates this beer, although the beer does mellow with keeping and there is enough malt body and fruitiness to make it more than one-dimensional. It is a beer that definitely requires slow, reflective sipping. Five gallons will last you a very long time, so the inclusion of a 1-barrel recipe must be very optimistic on my part!

American Amber Ales

Amber Waves of Grain

Malt	Extract 5 Gal.	All-Grain 5 Gal.	All-Grain 1 Bbl.
Amber malt syrup	3.0 lb. (1.36 kg) (48.4%)	—	—
Pale dry malt extract	1.7 lb. (772 g) (27.4%)	—	—
U.S. two-rowed			
pale malt	—	6.0 lb. (2.72 kg) (80.0%)	33.4 lb. (15.2 kg) (77.7%)
Munich malt	1.0 lb. (454 g) (16.1%)	1.0 lb. (454 g) (13.3%)	6.4 lb. (2.9 kg) (14.9%)
140 °L crystal malt	0.5 lb. (227 g) (8.1%)	0.5 lb. (227 g) (6.7%)	3.2 lb. (1.45 kg) (7.4%)
Beer color (°SRM)	21	19	19

Hops	Extract 5 Gal.	All-Grain 5 Gal.	All-Grain 1 Bbl.
Bittering Hops			
Chinook hop pellets			
(12.1% AA)	0.75 oz. (21 g)	0.6 oz. (17 g)	2.9 oz. (82 g)
HBU	92	7.3	—
IBU	27	27	27
Aroma Hops			
Willamette hop			
pellets (end of boil)	1.0 oz. (28 g)	1.0 oz. (28 g)	6.0 oz. (170 g)

Specifications

Original gravity:	1.045 (11.2 °P)
Final gravity:	1.009–1.011 (2.3–2.8 °P)
Water treatment:	Calcium 50–100 ppm; sulfate 100–200 ppm; chloride 20 ppm
Mash temperature:	152 °F (66.7 °C)
Yeast:	Wyeast 1056 American Ale
Alcohol v/v:	4.7% approximately
Serve:	Draught or bottle
Priming:	5.0–6.0 oz. (140–170 g) cane sugar
CO_2 v/v:	2.0–2.5

Pale Ale

This beer has quite a deep red-amber color and a complex caramel flavor from the use of both Munich and dark crystal malts. It has a fair malt body and relatively low, although definite, hop bitterness, with a nice spicy touch from the aroma hops.

American Pale Ales

Squeaky Clean

Malt	Extract 5 Gal.	All-Grain 5 Gal.	All-Grain 1 Bbl.
Pale malt syrup	6.0 lb. (2.72 kg) (88.9%)	—	—
Pale dry malt extract	0.75 lb. (341 g) (11.1%)	—	—
U.S. two-rowed pale malt	—	8.25 lb. (3.75 kg) (100%)	45.7 lb. (20.75 kg) (100%)
Beer color (°SRM)	5	4	4

Hops	Extract 5 Gal.	All-Grain 5 Gal.	All-Grain 1 Bbl.
Bittering Hops			
Willamette hop pellets (4.8% AA)	2.8 oz. (80 g)	2.0 oz. (57 g)	10.8 oz. (307 g)
HBU	13.4	9.6	—
IBU	40	40	40
Aroma Hops			
Willamette hop pellets (15 min.)	0.5 oz. (14 g)	0.5 oz. (14 g)	3.0 oz. (85 g)
Willamette hop pellets (end of boil)	1.0 oz. (28 g)	1.0 oz. (28 g)	6.0 oz. (170 g)

Specifications

Original gravity:	1.050 (12.4 °P)
Final gravity:	1.010–1.013 (2.6–3.3 °P)
Water treatment:	Calcium 50–100 ppm; sulfate 100–200 ppm; chloride 20 ppm
Mash temperature:	153–154 °F (67.2–67.3 °C)
Yeast:	Wyeast 1056 American Ale
Alcohol v/v:	5.1% approximately
Serve:	Draught or bottle
Priming:	5.0–6.0 oz. (140–170 g) cane sugar
CO_2 v/v:	2.0–2.5

Pale Ale

This is a very simple, straightforward beer, with no caramel malts and a fairly neutral yeast adding little in the way of fruitiness. The high mash temperature does give some malt body, and the late-hopped Willamette lends a nice spiciness to back off a fairly high level of bitterness. It is a single varietal hop beer, and with only one malt, the derivation of the name is obvious.

Tierra Bravado Pale Ale

Malt	Extract 5 Gal.	All-Grain 5 Gal.	All-Grain 1 Bbl.
Pale malt syrup	4.0 lb. (1.82 kg) (60.2%)	—	—
Pale dry malt extract	2.4 lb. (1.1 kg) (36.1%)	—	—
U.S. two-rowed pale malt	—	8.5 lb. (3.9 kg) (97.1%)	46.4 lb. (21.1 kg) (96.7%)
10 °L crystal malt	4.0 oz. (114 g) (3.8%)	4.0 oz. (114 g) (2.9%)	1.6 lb. (726 g) (3.3%)
Beer color (°SRM)	5	5	4

Hops	Extract 5 Gal.	All-Grain 5 Gal.	All-Grain 1 Bbl.
Bittering Hops			
Cascade hop flowers (5.7% AA)	2.0 oz. (57 g)	1.4 oz. (40 g)	7.5 oz. (213 g)
HBU	11.4	8.0	—
IBU	31	30	30
Aroma Hops			
Cascade hop flowers (30 min.)	0.5 oz. (14 g)	0.5 oz. (14 g)	3.0 oz. (85 g)
Cascade hop flowers (10 min.)	0.5 oz. (14 g)	0.5 oz. (14 g)	3.0 oz. (85 g)
Cascade hop flowers (end of boil)	1.0 oz. (28 g)	1.0 oz. (28 g)	6.0 oz. (170 g)

Specifications

Original gravity:	1.052 (12.9 °P)
Final gravity:	1.011–1.013 (2.8–3.3 °P)
Water treatment:	Calcium 100 ppm; sulfate 200 ppm, chloride 30 ppm
Mash temperature:	151 °F (66.1 °C)
Yeast:	Brewtek CL-10 American Microbrewery Ale #1
Alcohol v/v:	5.3% approximately
Serve:	Draught or bottle
Priming:	5.0–6.0 oz. (140–170 g) cane sugar
CO_2 v/v:	2.0–2.5

Pale Ale

This brew is very clean-tasting and very pale, thanks to the neutral yeast and just a touch of lightly roasted crystal. The dominant flavors are from the liberal use of Cascades aroma hops, with their characteristic, and quite unmistakable, flowery nature. Bitterness is intensified somewhat by moving to higher levels of minerals in the water. The name is a play on a well-known craft-brewed pale ale and could roughly be translated as "Land of the Brave."

American IPAS

New Edition IPA

Malt	Extract 5 Gal.	All-Grain 5 Gal.	All-Grain 1 Bbl.
Pale malt syrup	6.0 lb. (2.72 kg) (66 1%)	—	—
Pale dry malt extract	1.2 lb. (545 g) (13.2%)	—	—
U.S. two-rowed pale malt	—	9.0 lb. (4.1 kg) (8.28%)	49.5 lb. (22.5 kg) (80.5%)
80 °L crystal malt	6.0 oz. (170 g) (4.1%)	6.0 oz. (170 g) (3.4%)	2.4 lb. (1.1 kg) (3.9%)
Munich malt	1.5 lb. (681 g) (16.5%)	1.5 lb. (681 g) (13.8%)	9.6 lb. (4.4 kg) (15.6%)
Beer color (°SRM)	14	14	13

Hops	Extract 5 Gal.	All-Grain 5 Gal.	All-Grain 1 Bbl.
Bittering Hops			
Mt. Hood hop pellets (5.0% AA)	3.4 oz. (97 g)	2.4 oz. (68 g)	13.0 oz. (369 g)
HBU	17.0	12.0	—
IBU	51	51	50
Aroma Hops			
Mt. Hood hop pellets (15 min.)	0.5 oz. (14 g)	0.5 oz. (14 g)	3.0 oz. (85 g)
Liberty hop pellets (end of boil)	0.5 oz. (14 g)	0.5 oz. (14 g)	3.0 oz. (85 g)
Liberty hop pellets (dry hop in secondary)	0.5 oz. (14 g)	0.5 oz. (14 g)	3.0 oz. (85 g)

Specifications

Original gravity:	1.065 (15.9 °P)
Final gravity:	1.013–1.016 (3.3–4.1 °P)
Water treatment:	Calcium 100 ppm; sulfate 200 ppm chloride 30 ppm
Mash temperature:	150 °F (65.6 °C)
Yeast:	Brewtek CL-20 American Microbrewery Ale #2
Alcohol v/v:	6.6% approximately
Serve:	Draught or bottle
Priming:	6.0–7.0 oz. (170–200 g) cane sugar
CO_2 v/v:	2.5 for draught; 2.5–3.0 for bottles

Pale Ale

This beer is many sided and strong in alcohol. It has good body with a fair amount of caramel in the background, lots of American hop character, and a high level of bitterness. However, the hop character, given a nice sharp edge from the dry-hopping, is gentle and spicy and not as aggressive as some other American hops. This is definitely a sipping rather than a quaffing beer. The title reflects the American craftbrewers return to the basics of traditional IPA, rather than the lesser compromise made by English commercial brewers.

Take the Ball and Run IPA

Malt	Extract 5 Gal.	All-Grain 5 Gal.	All-Grain 1 Bbl.
Pale malt syrup	6.0 lb. (2.72 kg) (65.2%)	—	—
Pale dry malt extract	2.7 lb. (1.2 kg) (29.4%)	—	—
U.S. two-rowed pale malt	—	11.25 lb. (5.1 kg) (95.7%)	61.7 lb. (28 kg) (95.1%)
40 °L crystal malt	6.0 oz. (170 g) (4.1%)	6.0 oz. (170 g) (3.2%)	2.4 lb. (1.1 kg) (3.7%)
140 °L crystal malt	2.0 oz. (57 g) (1.4%)	2.0 oz. (57 g) (1.1%)	0.8 lb. (363 g) (1.3%)
Beer color (°SRM)	12	12	11

Hops	Extract 5 Gal.	All-Grain 5 Gal.	All-Grain 1 Bbl.
Bittering Hops			
Cascade hop pellets (5.7% AA)	3.5 oz. (99 g)	2.5 oz. (71 g)	13.6 oz. (386 g)
HBU	20.0	14.3	—
IBU	60	60	60
Aroma Hops			
Cascade hop pellets (30 min.)	1.0 oz. (23 g)	1.0 oz. (28 g)	6.0 oz. (170 g)
Cascade hop pellets (15 min.)	1.0 oz. (23 g)	1.0 oz. (28 g)	6.0 oz. (170 g)
Cascade hop pellets (end of boil)	1.0 oz. (23 g)	1.0 oz. (28 g)	6.0 oz. (170 g)
Cascade hop pellets (dry hop in secondary)	0.5 oz. (14 g)	0.5 oz. (14 g)	3.0 oz. (85 g)

Specifications

Original gravity:	1.070 (17.1 °P)
Final gravity:	1.013–1.017 (3.3–4.3 °P)
Water treatment:	Calcium 150–200 ppm; sulfate 300–400 ppm; chloride 30 ppm
Mash temperature:	150 °F (65.6 °C)
Yeast:	Wyeast 1272 American Ale II
Alcohol v/v:	7.3% approximately
Serve:	Draught or bottle
Priming:	6.0–7.0 oz. (170–200 g) cane sugar
CO_2 v/v:	2.0–3.0

Pale Ale

This is an IPA with character coming out everywhere. It offers plenty of alcohol and lots of malt character, with both the yeast and the crystal malt adding nutty notes, and a high level of bitterness to balance it all out. However, it has the liberal use of aroma hops that means the powerful flowery fragrance of Cascades is really dominant—it might be over the top for some drinkers! The name reflects the fact that American craftbrewers have not just revived traditional IPA values—they have gone a step further and created a new style.

Recommended
Commercial
Pale Ales

It seems appropriate to make some comments about examples of this style, but I can do this only on a limited scale. This is not a beer guide. It would take another book, at least, to cover the many examples available in England and America. Also, I certainly cannot claim to have drunk all examples of the style available in these two countries, although I have taken a good shot at it! I recommend the *CAMRA Beer Guide 1997* from CAMRA Books (the 1998 version should be out by the time this book is published). It offers information on British breweries and pubs that serve cask-conditioned bitters and pale ales. Also, I recommend the CAMRA *Guide to Real Ale in a Bottle* by Jeff Evans (St.

Albans, England: CAMRA Books, 1997), which might be useful if you are visiting England and want to take home some of the real stuff.

America has nothing as comprehensive as the CAMRA guide. This is not surprising, since it has no organization like CAMRA and it is a much bigger country to cover. A number of attempts have been made by various authors. Of these, I recommend Steve Johnson's *America's Best Brews* (Houston: Gulf Publishing Company, 1997). I also recommend the following On Tap books by Steve Johnson: *On Tap Guide to North American Brewpubs* (Clemson, South Carolina: WBR Publications, 1993); *Vol. I U.S. East of the Mississippi and Canada, Vol. II U.S. West of the Mississippi*, and *On Tap New England* (Clemson, South Carolina: WBR Publications, 1994). The best I can do here is to suggest a few examples of the styles you might look out for.

English Examples

If you go to London, England, try the brews from the two independents, Young's and Fuller's. In particular, look for **Young's Special Bitter** and **Fuller's London Pride**, two best bitters that are hard to beat when at their best! And of course **Fuller's ESB** is an outstanding special bitter. West of London, look for Brakspear's of Henley. Its bitter is an excellent example of just how much flavor can be

The Flower Pots Inn's origins as a house are obvious. It's just the place to slake a thirst generated by cycling around the hilly Hampshire countryside.

squeezed from a low-gravity ordinary bitter. Very similar in strength and also very flavorful is **Best Bitter** from Hook, Norton in Oxfordshire. Another favorite of mine comes from the Salisbury microbrewer Hop Back. Its **Summer Lighting**, a top-end best bitter, is very hoppy indeed, yet it is a surprisingly easy-drinking beer.

Harder to find is **Pots Ale**, a very bitter, hoppy ordinary bitter. It is brewed at the Cheriton Brewhouse in Hampshire, right in the yard of a delightful country pub, the Flower Pots Inn. Perhaps some of the hoppiest cask-conditioned bitters are those from the Bishops Brewery, based appropriately enough around the corner from the

Hop Exchange, in Southwark. This was where the first Flemish beer brewers settled; they introduced hops to England in the fifteenth century. The brewery itself is not too far from the new Globe Theatre, a reconstruction of the one at which many of Shakespeare's plays were first staged. Get yer Hampsteads around a pint of **Cathedral Bitter**, and then go and see the Bard's work much as it was originally performed, in an open theatre, but not, of course, in winter! What are Hampsteads? Hampstead Heaths (don't pronounce the H) are teeth in Cockney rhyming slang!

On the East Coast, you have to look for Adnam's in Suffolk. In particular, its **Best Bitter** (actually an ordinary) and **Broadside** (a best) are very enjoyable, although another best, **Extra**, is the championship winner of the three. The brewery is right by the coast in the charming little town of Southwold (where the writer George Orwell once lived). The beers there have an unusual flavor, sometimes said to be redolent of seaweed. Not far away is the town of Norwich. This is where the micro Woodforde brews; it has no fewer than two former Champion Beers of Britain in its portfolio. Try its **Wherry Best Bitter** for an ordinary with a lot of hop bitterness and aromatic character.

In the Midlands area, try Marston's, a Burton brewer, although you can find their pubs and beers over a wide area. **Pedigree** is the only English beer still brewed in Unions. When kept well, it is an excellent best bitter, with the good hop bitterness, nice maltiness, and good dry finish that a Burton pale ale should have. Some of its bottled beers are sold in America including its **India Export Pale Ale**, which I found pleasant but somewhat blander than expected. Bass, of course, still brews in Burton, but without the Unions. Its beer, **Draught Bass**, is a best bitter that can rarely be found in good shape these days. It is, to me, disappointingly bland.

Quite a few northern beers are worthy of note, particularly those from Timothy Taylor, a Yorkshire brewer. Its **Landlord**, a best bitter and a former Champion Beer of Britain, is a long-time favorite of mine. It is both interesting and dangerously drinkable—hoppy, fruity, and malty with an unusual nutty aspect. From the same county comes Samuel Smith, whose only real ale is **Old Brewery Bitter**. This, and its bottled **Pale Ale**, which is widely available in America, are good examples of beers produced in Yorkshire stone squares. They exhibit a characteristic buttery note, derived from diacetyl. The Yorkshire micro Barnsley Brewery offers an IPA, although its gravity puts it only in the best bitter range. Yet I found this to be one of the hoppiest beers that I have tried in a while in terms of both a lovely grassy, lemony aroma and a hefty bitterness. On a short visit to England, you might not have

A pub owned by one of Britain's largest brewers. The sign is more interesting than the beer!

time to locate it, but the taste of this beer will well repay you for hunting for it.

In Manchester and the Northwest area are a number of good ordinary bitters. Those from Cain's in Liverpool, Manchester's Holt's, and Hyde's Anvil are worth looking for, while the Cumbrian brewer, Jennings, offers a couple of unusually dark bitters. One of these rejoices in the name of **Sneck Lifter**—and you can make what you like of that! One of the archetypal pale, very bitter ordinary bitters I used to associate with Manchester is **Boddington's**. Whitbread now owns and operates the ex-Boddington brewery and has somewhat emasculated the beer in its efforts to make it a national brand. Boddington's is available in America as "pub beer" in cans fitted with the nitrogen "widget." This means that it pours with a creamy head but has a low carbon dioxide content. It still has the very pale color I always knew and a not bad hoppy bitterness, but it no longer has the sharp bite of old.

There are many others I could mention. One is **Deuchars IPA** (really an ordinary bitter) from Caledonian in Scotland, which is sold in bottle in America. And there are some good brewers in Wales, such as Felinfoel and its unusual **Double Dragon** (a best bitter), as well as **Brains**. The latter's beers are not particularly distinctive, but with advertising slogans like "Get Some Brains," it is worth mentioning. Of course, there are quite a few British beers on sale in America, but they are all either bottled or kegged and not at all the same as when tasted in cask-conditioned form on their home territory. If you are really interested in this style, you should make the effort to cross the water at some stage in your brewing career.

American Examples

As for American brews in the genre, there are, happily, many more than I could hope to deal with here. Some are now old favorites and were mentioned earlier in the book. These include **Sierra Nevada Pale Ale** (a little too clean and lacking in complexity for my taste, but it is a classic of its kind) and **Ballantine's IPA**. Although not quite the beer it used to be, Ballantine's is still not a bad drink. **Bert Grant's IPA** remains a very bitter but still malty version of the American IPA style, as does **Anchor's Liberty Ale**.

Geary's of Portland, Maine, does a nice pale ale. It's nicely bitter but has more of the nutty, caramel character of the English style of pale ale.

Full Sail from Oregon has an excellent IPA, although this is really an English version, since it uses East Kent Goldings. The same brewery does a good, quite bitter and unusually strong amber ale. Rogue, also from Oregon, has an excellent **American Amber Ale** that is hoppy and has a nice caramel flavor. And Catamount in Vermont is still turning out its **Amber Ale**. It is perhaps something of a transition beer, but it is still nicely balanced and has a definite bitterness.

The Commonwealth Brewery, a Boston brewpub, now offers **Boston Burton Ale** in bottles (actually brewed by Catamount under license). This is a nicely balanced beer, fruity and nutty with good hop bitterness. Also from Boston is Mass. Bay Brewing's **Harpoon IPA**. An excellent version of the style, it

A new-era pale ale and IPA, brewed in Maine and Boston, Massachusetts, respectively. Both more in the English rather than American style, but well hopped and bitter as they should be.

has plenty of malt, good hop character, and bitterness, as well as a nice fruity background. Redhook, now brewing on both coasts, offers an ESB that has much of the malty character of the original. A very hoppy East Coast brew is Brooklyn Brewing's **East India Pale Ale**. It uses some slightly odd ingredients, such as Pilsener and wheat malts, but along with English pale malt and a mixture of English and American hops. In terms of both strength and flavor, it is most definitely a return to basics, in the sense of reproducing the original IPA flavor.

Some beers that are relatively local to me also fit these categories. New England's **Amber Ale**, with its fresh, powerful Cascades hop character, could be classed as more of an IPA, although the brewery has recently brought out an IPA also. And Bank Street Brewery, a brewpub in Stamford, Connecticut, offers a tantalizingly complex, malty, and bitter **Banker's Bitter**, whose strength would put it in the IPA class, rather than the bitter class. In the Northeast are a few breweries offering cask-conditioned ale, with the most notable being Emerald Isle out of Rhode Island. But none of its outlets are close enough for me to make it a local.

The beer scene in America is still quite fragmented. Many of the craft beers are not available to drinkers unless you are prepared to travel quite a distance, particularly when you are looking at draught beers. It even seems that

I had to include a picture of the Ship Inn, a brewpub, because it is in Milford, New Jersey, which is as close as I can get to a brewpub from where I live in Milford, Connecticut.

the choice in liquor stores has recently become much narrower. This is why I do not list any more beers. Also, because I am less familiar with West Coast beers than I am with those on the East Coast, I have mentioned only a few of them. I urge you to get out and see what is available and sample them yourself.

We are still not where I would like us to be in America in terms of distribution of both brewpubs and pubs serving craft beers. Only a few big cities have the luxury of a wide choice of beers and of pubs serving them. I can get decent beer in the town where I live, but the choice is pretty limited, and I have none serving anything more than a couple of nonindustrial beers on draught. And the nearest brewpub is at least a 25-minute drive away. If only somebody would open one in Milford, Connecticut.

Suggested Reading

Malt Extract Selection

1. "American Homebrewers Association Survey of Hop Content," *Zymurgy* (Spring 1986): 22. (No author given in article.)
2. Norman Farrell, "The Enchanting World of Malt Extract," *Zymurgy* (Winter 1994): 34–41.
3. "Maltsters and Malt Products from around the World," in *The 1997 Brewers' Market Guide* (Eugene, Ore.: New Wine Press, Inc., 1997), 71–96, 108–110.
4. Bill Metzger, "Extracting the Essentials," *Zymurgy* (Summer 1996): 36–42.
5. Charlie Papazian, "Brewing Techniques Influence Bitterness," *Zymurgy* (Winter 1985): 30–31.

6. Jill Singleton, "AHA Definitive Guide, The Lowdown on Malt Extracts," *Zymurgy* (Special Issue 1986): 22–23.

Malt Analysis

1. Gregory J. Noonan, "Making Sense of a Malt Analysis," *Zymurgy* (Special Issue 1995): 15–16.
2. Gregory J. Noonan, "Understanding Malt Analysis Sheets— How to Become Fluent in Malt Analysis Interpretation," in *The 1997 Brewers' Market Guide* (Eugene, Ore.: New Wine Press, Inc., 1997), 115–119.
3. Gregory J. Noonan, *New Brewing Lager Beer* (Boulder, Colo.: Brewers Publications, 1996), 7–23.

Methods for Preparation of Crystal Malt

1. Randy Mosher, *The Brewers Companion* (Seattle: Alephenalia Publications, 1994), 137.
2. Randy Mosher, "Roast, Roast, Roast Your Grains," *Zymurgy* (Summer 1998): 42–44.
3. Charlie Papazian, *The Complete Joy of Home Brewing* (New York: Avon Books, 1994), 207.

Barley-Based Syrups

1. Ted Bruning, "Syrup Firms Invest for the Future," *Brewers' Guardian* (December 1993): 12–13.

2. Tim O'Rourke and David Pierpoint, "Developments in the Use of Brewing Adjuncts in Britain," *Brewers Guardian* (July 1994): 17, 18, 20, 21.
3. Graham G. Stewart, "Adjuncts," in *Handbook of Brewing* (New York: Marcel Dekker, 1995), 127–129.
4. Trevor Wainwright, "Using Sugar Adjuncts in Brewing," *Brewers' Guardian* (December 1993): 14, 16, 17, 29.

Hop Varieties

1. Jim Busch, "How to Master Hop Character," *Brewing Techniques* (January/February 1997): 30–33.
2. Ray Daniels, "Hop Physiology and Chemistry," *Zymurgy* (Special Issue 1997): 40–47.
3. George Fix, *Principles of Brewing Science* (Boulder, Colo.: Brewers Publications, 1989), 48–58.
4. George J. Fix and Laurie A. Fix, *An Analysis of Brewing Techniques* (Boulder, Colo.: Brewers Publications, 1997), 33–34.
5. Mark Garetz, "Hop Storage," *Brewing Techniques* (January/February 1994): 26–32.
6. Mark Garetz, *Using Hops* (Danville, Calif.: HopTech, 1994).
7. Michael Hall, "IBU," *Zymurgy* (Special Issue, 1997): 76.
8. Alfred Haunold and Gail B. Nickerson, "Factors Affecting Hop Production, Hop Quality and Brewer Preference," *Brewing Techniques* (May/June 1993): 18–24.
9. Gerard W. Ch. Lemmens, "The Breeding and Parentage of Hop Varieties," *Brewers Digest* (May 1993): 16–26.

10. W. C. Lemmens, "Hop Utilization," *American Brewer* (Spring 1993): 29–35.

11. Michael Moir, "The Chemistry of Hop Flavours," *Brewers' Guardian* (December 1987): 7–11.

12. Don Put, "The Pursuit of Hoppiness, Part II," *Brewing Techniques* (May/June 1996): 18–23.

13. Glenn Tinseth, "The Essential Oil of Hops," *Brewing Techniques* (January/February 1994): 33–37.

Traditional Fermenters

1. Michael J. Lewis and Tom W. Young, *Brewing* (London: Chapman and Hall, 1995), 163–170.

Yeast Strain Selection

1. Patrick Weix, "Become Saccharomyces Savvy," *Zymurgy* (Summer 1994): 48–49.

Yeast Cultures

1. Jim Busch, "Some Finer Points in Preparing Wort and Yeast for Fermentation," *Brewing Techniques* (September/October 1995): 26–31.

2. Paul Farnsworth, "Healthy Homebrew Starter Cultures," *Zymurgy* (Special Issue 1989): 10–13.

3. Paul Farnsworth, "Yeast Stock Maintenance and Starter Culture Production," *Zymurgy* (Special Issue 1989): 32–35.

4. Rog Leistad, *Yeast Culturing for the Homebrewers* (Ann Arbor, Mich.: G. W. Kent, 1983).

5. Dave Miller, "Getting a Lift from Your Yeast," *Zymurgy* (Fall 1988): 35–38.

6. Randy Mosher, *The Brewer's Companion* (Seattle: Alephenalia Publications, 1994), 187–192.

7. Pierre Rajotte, *First Steps in Yeast Culture, Part One* (Montreal: Alliage Editeur, 1994).

Brewing Water Chemistry

1. George J. and Laurie A. Fix, *An Analysis of Brewing Techniques* (Boulder, Colo.: Brewers Publications, 1997). 14–22.

2. Gregory J. Noonan, *New Brewing Lager Beer* (Boulder, Colo.: Brewers Publications, 1996), 35–76.

Counterpressure Bottling

1. David Ruggiero, Jonathan Spillane, and Doug Snyder, "The Counterpressure Connection," *Zymurgy* (Fall 1995): 56–63.

Handling and Selection of Kegs

1. Kirk R. Fleming, "Discover the Joys of Kegging," *Brewing Techniques* (January/February 1997): 22–29.

2. Ed Westemeier, "A Bottler's Guide to Kegging," *Zymurgy* (Summer 1995): 46–53.

Brewing Real Ale

1. Jim Busch, "Cask Conditioning Ales at Home," *Brewing Techniques* (November/December 1995): 30–35.
2. Dick Cantwell, Fal Allen, and Kevin Forhan, "Beer from the Stainless," *Brewing Techniques* (November/December 1993): 22–28.
3. Ivor Clissold, *Cellarmanship* (St. Albans, England: CAMRA Books, 1997).
4. Mark Dorber, "Cellarmanship," *All About Beer* (July 1997): 22–25.
5. Sal Emma, "Cask Conditioned Ale," *Brew Your Own* (May 1997): 38–45.
6. Benjamin Myers, "Cellarmen: Heroes of the Real Ale Revolution," *All About Beer* (May 1994): 2–22, 42–43.

Where to Find Real Ale

1. Fal Allen, "Beer Thrall," *American Brewer*, no. 77 (1998): 39.
2. Ray Daniels, "Beer from the Wood," *All About Beer* (July 1997): 14–17, 20.
3. Ray Daniels, "Real Ale," *Zymurgy* (Spring 1997): 44–51.
4. Stan Hieronymous, "Fresh from the Cask," *All About Beer* (September 1995): 12–13.
5. Stan Hieronymous and Daria Labinsky, "Real Ale on the Road," *All About Beer* (July 1997): 70–71.
6. Benjamin Myers, "Cask Ale Crosses the Atlantic," *All About Beer* (May 1994): 21.

Source of Suppliers

1. *Brewers' Market Guide* (Eugene, Ore.: New Wine Press, Inc., 1998), 135–140, 142–144.
2. Jim Busch, "Cask Conditioning Ales at Home," *Brewing Techniques* (November/December 1995): 34.
3. Dick Cantwell, Fal Allen, and Kevin Forhan, "Beer from the Stainless," *Brewing Techniques* (November/December 1993): 34.
4. Jason Dunson-Todd, "Beer from the Wood," *Brewing Techniques* (September 1997): 68.

Chapter Notes

Chapter 1: The Evolution of Pale Ale

1. Dr. John Harrison, "Capturing the flavour of beers gone by," *Brewers Guardian* (November 1995): 48–53.
2. John Bickerdyke, *The Curiosities of Ale and Beer* (1889; reprint, London: Spring Books, 1989), 79.
3. Jeffrey Patton, *Additives, Adulterants and Contaminants in Beer* (North Devon, England: Patton Publications, 1899); 6–9.
4. Pamela Sambrook, *Country House Brewing in England* (London: Hambledon Press, 1996), 13.
5. H. S. Corran, *A History of Brewing* (London: David and Charles, 1975), 134.
6. John Tuck, *Private Brewer's Guide to the Art of Brewing Ale and Porter* (1822; reprint, Zymoscribe, Conn.: 1995), 139–141.
7. Corran, *A History of Brewing*, 80.
8. "Coke," *Kirk-Othmer Encyclopedia of Chemical Technology*, Vol. 6, Fourth Edition (New York: John Wiley and Son), 1993.
9. Sambrook, *Country House Brewing in England*, 128–129.
10. Peter Mathias, *The Brewing Industry in England 1700–1830* (reprint, Aldershot, England: Gregg Revivals, 1959), 150.
11. Bass Museum Burton-on-Trent, personal notes by author.
12. Mathias, *The Brewing Industry in England 1700–1830*, 6.

13. Corran, *A History of Brewing*, 79.
14. Ibid., 113.
15. Hurford Janes, *The Red Barrel: A History of Watney Mann* (London: John Murray, 1963), 15.
16. Mathias, *The Brewing Industry of England 1700–1830*, 12.
17. Colin C. Owen, *The Greatest Brewery in the World: A History of Bass, Ratcliffe, & Gretton* (Chesterfield, England: The Derbyshire Record Society, 1992), 13–14.
18. R. Gourvish and R. G. Wilson, *The British Brewing Industry 1830–1980* (Cambridge: Cambridge University Press, 1994), 90.
19. Janes, *The Red Barrel: A History of Watney Mann*, 61–62.
20. Thom Thomlinson, "Brewing in Styles: India Pale Ale, Part I," *Brewing Techniques* (March/April 1994): 24.
21. Mathias, *The Brewing Industry in England 1700–1830*, 189.
22. Harrison, "Capturing the flavour of beers gone by," 48–50.
23. *Old British Beers and How to Make Them* (Durden Park, England: Durden Park Beer Circle, 1991), 26.
24. "Meeting Report: British Guild of Beer Writers India Pale Ale Conference"; "Ale and a passage to India," *What's Brewing* (July 1994): 8–9.
25. Ibid., 491.
26. "Meeting Report: British Guild of Beer Writers India Pale Ale Conference," *Brewing Techniques* (July/August 1994): 12.
27. Mathias, *The Brewing Industry in England 1700–1830*, 184–185.

28. Meredith Brown, *The Brewer's Art* (London: Whitbread & Co., 1948), 51.

29. Mathias, *The Brewing Industry in England 1700–1830*, 185.

30. Owen, *The Greatest Brewery in the World: A History of Bass, Ratcliffe, & Gretton*, 30.

31. Mathias, *The Brewing Industry in England 1700–1830*, 189.

32. Dr. Trevor Wainwright, "The origin, decline, and revival of India Pale Ale," *Brewer's Guardian* (October 1994): 40–41.

33. Martyn Cornell, "Mass slaughter of the innocents," *What's Brewing* (1997): 12–13.

34. Gourvish and Wilson, *The British Brewing Industry 1830–1980*, 90.

35. Tomlinson, "Brewing in Styles: India Pale Ale, Part I," 24; Cornell, "Mass slaughter of the innocents," 12.

36. "Ale and a passage to India," 9.

37. *A Visit to Bass' Brewery* (reprint 1902, Burton-on-Trent: Bass Museum, 1977), 4.

38. Mathias, *The Brewing Industry in England 1700–1830*, 184–185.

39. Owen, *The Greatest Brewery in the World: A History of Bass, Ratcliffe, & Gretton*, 38.

40. Mathias, *The Brewing Industry in England 1700–1830*, 192.

41. Jeff Evans, *The CAMRA Guide to Real Ale in a Bottle* (St. Albans, England: CAMRA Books, 1997), 14.

42. "Lord of the jungle abandons heritage," *What's Brewing* (January 1998): 4.

43. Owen, *The Greatest Brewery in the World: A History of Bass, Ratcliffe, & Gretton*, 49.

44. "Ale and a passage to India," 8.

45. "Ale and a passage to India," 8.

46. Gourvish and Wilson, *The British Brewing Industry 1830–1980*, 30.

47. Ibid., 25.

48. Ibid., 65–72.

49. H. Hawkins and C. L. Pass, *The Brewing Industry* (London: Heinemann, 1979), 22.

50. Owen, *The Greatest Brewery in the World: A History of Bass, Ratcliffe, & Gretton*, 49.

51. Mark Sturley, *The Breweries and Public Houses of Guildford* (Guildford: Charles W. Traylen, 1990), 162.

52. Sambrook, *Country House Brewing in England*, 70.

53. Owen, *The Greatest Brewery in the World: A History of Bass, Ratcliff, & Gretton*, 49.

54. Gourvish and Wilson, *The British Brewing Industry 1830–1980*, 94–95.

55. Owen, *The Greatest Brewery in the World: A History of Bass, Ratcliffe, & Gretton*, 226, 235.

56. Owen, *The Greatest Brewery in the World: A History of Bass, Ratcliffe, & Gretton*, 53.

57. Wainwright, "The origin, decline and fall of India Pale Ale," 40.

58. Gourvish and Wilson, *The British Brewing Industry 1830–1980*, 50.

59. Ibid., 10.

60. Brian Bennison, *Brewers and Bottlers of Newcastle upon Tyne From 1850 to the present day* (Newcastle upon Tyne:

Community & Leisure Services Department, City
Libraries & Arts, 1995), 8–9.

61. Bass Museum Burton-on-Trent, personal notes by author.

62. Owen, *The Greatest Brewery in the World: A History of
Bass, Ratcliffe, & Gretton*, 73.

63. Ibid., 124–125.

64. Graham Lees, "Stylistically Speaking: Märzen," *All About
Beer* (November 1996), 64.

65. John Richards, *A History of Holden's Black Country Brewery*
(Swinton, Manchester, England: Neil Richardson, 1986), 7.

66. Ibid., 7.

67. Owen, *The Greatest Brewery in the World: A History of
Bass, Ratcliffe, & Gretton*, 52.

68. Corran, *A History of Brewing*, 209.

69. Charles Graham, "On Lager Beer," *Chemistry and Industry*
(1881): 9.

70. Garrett Oliver, "Stylistically Speaking: East India Pale
Ale," *All About Beer* (March 1995): 62.

71. Robert Wahl and Max Henius, *American Handy Book of
the Brewing, Malting, and Auxiliary Trades* (Chicago: Wahl-
Henius Institute, 1908), 1284.

72. Roger Protz, "Malt: The Soul of Beer," *All About Beer* (September 1996), 41.

73. Owen, *The Greatest Brewery in the World: A History of
Bass, Ratcliffe, & Gretton*, 23.

74. Tim O'Rourke and David Pierpoint, 'Developments in the
use of brewing adjuncts in Britain," *Brewer's Guardian*
(July 1994): 17–21.

75. Jonathon Brown, *Steeped in Tradition*, University of Reading Institute of Agricultural History Museum of English Rural Life (1983): 26.

76. Harrison, "Capturing the flavor of beers gone by," 49.

77. Gourvish and Wilson, *The British Brewing Industry 1830–1980*, 56; "Ale and a passage to India," 8.

78. Tuck, *Private Brewer's Guide to the Art of Brewing Ale and Porter*, 139–141.

79. Owen, *The Greatest Brewery in the World: A History of Bass, Ratcliffe, & Gretton*, 71.

80. Tuck, *Private Brewer's Guide to the Art of Brewing Ale and Porter*, 139–141.

81. "Ale and a passage to India," 24.

82. Graham Wheeler, "Turning pale at thought of a genuine India ale," *What's Brewing* (July 1994): 30.

83. Alfred Barnard, *Bass & Co. Limited*, as described in *Noted Breweries of Great Britain & Ireland* (1887 reprint, Burton-on-Trent: Bass Museum, 1977): 46–47.

84. Owen, *The Greatest Brewery in the World: A History of Bass, Ratcliffe, & Gretton*, 62.

85. Ibid., 75.

86. Ibid., 114; Gourvish and Wilson, *The British Brewing Industry 1830–1980*, 185.

87. Graham, "On Lager Beer," 24.

88. Tomlinson, "Brewing in Styles: India Pale Ale, Part I," 26.

89. Martin D. Walker and William J. Simpson, "Control of sulphery [sic] flavours in cask conditioned beer," *Brewer's Guardian* (November 1994): 38.

90. Bass Museum, *A Visit to Bass' Brewery*, 31.

91. Thom Tomlinson, "Brewing in Styles: India Pale Ale, Part II," *Brewing Techniques* (May/June 1994): 20.

92. Michael Jackson, *Michael Jackson's Beer Companion* (Philadelphia: Running Press, 1993), 96.

93. Owen, *The Greatest Brewery in the World: A History of Bass, Ratcliffe, & Gretton*, 83.

94. Wheeler, "Turning pale at thought of a genuine India ale," 30.

95. Cornell, "Mass slaughter of the innocents," 13.

96. Gourvish and Wilson, *The British Brewing Industry 1830–1980*, 50.

97. Ibid., 184.

98. Owen, *The Greatest Brewery in the World: A History of Bass, Ratcliffe, & Gretton*, 88.

99. Ibid., 183.

100. O'Rourke and Pierpoint, "Developments in the use of brewing adjuncts in Britain," 17.

101. Brown, *Steeped in Tradition*, 27.

102. Owen, *The Greatest Brewery in the World: A History of Bass, Ratcliffe, & Gretton*, 147, 153.

103. "Don't punish the pint," *What's Brewing* (November 1993): 1.

104. Gourvish and Wilson, *The British Brewing Industry 1830–1980*, 229, 300; Owen, *The Greatest Brewery in the World: A History of Bass, Ratcliffe, & Gretton*, 109.

105. Graham, "On Lager Beer," 20.

106. Michael Jackson, *The New World Guide to Beer* (Philadelphia: Running Press, 1988), 165.

107. John Richards, *The History of Batham's Black Country Brewers* (Dudley, West Midlands: Real Ale Books, 1993), 1.

108. Corran, *A History of Brewing*, 216.

109. Keith Osborne, *Bygone Breweries* (Rochester, Kent: Rochester Press, 1982), 21, 48.

110. Richards, *The History of Holden's Black Country Brewery*, 6.

111. Bennison, *Brewers and Bottlers of Newcastle upon Tyne*, 8, 10.

112. Sturley, *The Breweries and Public Houses of Guildford*, 57, 60, 71; Graham, "On Lager Beer," 20.

113. Gourvish and Wilson, *The British Brewing Industry 1830–1980*, 558.

114. Graham, "On Lager Beer," 19.

115. Jeff Evans, ed., *Good Beer Guide* (St. Albans, England: CAMRA, 1998), 417–529.

116. Helen Osborn, forthcoming book on the history of Young's Brewery.

117. Ian Mackey, "New Brewery Statistics," *Brewery History Society Newsletter*, no. 17 (September 1997): 15.

118. Stanley Baron, *Brewed in America* (New York: Little, Brown and Company, 1962), 123.

119. Ibid., 188.

120. Michael Jackson, "Will the Americans help us discover our IPA heritage?," *Brewer's Guardian* (June 1994): 13.

121. Thom Tomlinson, "Response to Letter," *Brewing Techniques* (November/December 1994): 14.

122. Sambrook, *Country House Brewing in England*, 77.

123. Martin Lodahl, "Brewing in Styles: Old, Strong, and Stock Ales," *Brewing Techniques* (September/October 1994): 24–25; David Brockington, "Brewing in Styles: The

Evolution and Contemporary Brewing of American IPA," *Brewing Techniques* (September/October 1996): 39–40.

124. Jackson, "Will the Americans help us discover our IPA heritage?," 13.

125. Andrew Langley, *London Pride* (Melksham, Wiltshire: Good Books, 1995), 54.

126. David Brockington, "Brewing in Styles: West Coast Amber Ale," *Brewing Techniques* (November/December 1995): 37–44.

Chapter 2: Style Definitions and Profiles of Pale Ales

1. H. Lloyd Hind, *Brewing Science and Practice* (New York: John Wiley & Sons Inc., 1938), 542–544.

2. Jean De Clerck, *A Textbook of Brewing* (London: Chapman & Hall Ltd., 1957), 556.

3. J. S. Hough, D. E. Briggs, R. Stevens, and T. W. Young, *Malting and Brewing Science, Volume I* (London: Chapman and Hall, 1971), 10, 317.

4. William A. Hardwick, Ed., *Handbook of Brewing* (New York: Marcel Dekker, 1995), 55.

5. W. Kunze, *Technology Brewing and Malting* (Berlin: VLB Berlin, 1996), 573.

6. Michael J. Lewis and Tom W. Young, *Brewing* (London: Chapman and Hall, 1995).

7. David Brockington, "The Evolution and Contemporary Brewing of American IPA,' *Brewing Techniques* (September/October 1996): 39.

8. Alan Moen, "The Last Wort," *Brewing Techniques* (September 1997): 98, 86, 87; Keith Thomas, "Beer Styles: An International Analysis," *Brewery History Journal* (Summer 1975): 35–40.

9. Evans, *Good Beer Guide*; Jeff Evans, *Guide to Real Ale in a Bottle* (St. Albans, England: CAMRA Books, 1997); Roger Protz, *The Real Ale Drinker's Almanac,* Third Edition (Glasgow: Neil Wilson Publishing Ltd., 1993); Hugh Madgin, *Best of British Bottled Beer* (Shepperton, England: Dial House, 1995).

10. "Style Guidelines Chart," *Zymurgy* 21, no. 1 (Spring 1998): 79.

11. Michael Jackson, *The New World Guide to Beer* (Philadelphia: Running Press, 1988), 148.

12. "White Shield is saved but cask fight goes on," *What's Brewing* (April 1998): 4.

13. Michael Jackson, *Michael Jackson's Beer Companion* (Philadelphia: Running Press, 1998), 73.

14. "Style Guidelines Chart," 79.

15. Tony Babinec and Steve Hamburg, "Confessions of Two Bitter Men," *Zymurgy* 18, no. 2 (Summer 1995): 36–43.

16. "Style Guidelines Chart." 79.

17. Steve Johnson, *America's Best Brews* (Houston: Gulf Publishing Company, 1997).

18. "Style Guidelines Chart," 79.

19. Stephen Mallery, "The Oregon Pale Ale Experiment, Parts I and II," *Brewing Techniques* (October/November 1997): 58–64.

20. "World Beers Reviewed," *All About Beer* (May 1998): 56.

21. Jackson, *The New World Guide to Beer*: Jackson, *Michael Jackson's Beer Companion*.

22. David Brockington, "West Coast Amber Ale," *Brewing Techniques* (November/December 1995), 36–44.

23. "Style Guidelines Chart," 79.

24. Weaver, "In Support of West Coast Amber," *Brewing Techniques* (May/June 1996): 16–17.

25. Ray Daniels, *Designing Great Beers* (Boulder, Colo.: Brewers Publications, 1996); Fred Eckhardt, *The Essentials of Beer Style* (Portland, Ore.: Fred Eckardt Associates, 1989).

Chapter 3: Brewing Pale Ales

1. George J. Fix and Laurie A. Fix, *An Analysis of Brewing Techniques* (Boulder, Colo.: Brewers Publications, 1997), 126–130; Todd Hanson, "Home Filtration and Carbonation" in *Beer and Brewing, Volume 7* (Boulder, Colo.: Brewers Publications, 1987), 93–109; Karl F. Lutzen and Mark Stevens, *Brew Ware* (Pownal, Vt.: Storey Publishing, 1996), 42–44; Ray Daniels, "How Clear Is Your Beer: Parts I and II," *Zymurgy* 20, no. 3 (Fall 1997): 28–31, 34–37, 93–96.

2. "Great Homebrewing Kits," *Brew Your Own* (October 1997): 40–49.

3. Martin Lodahl, "Malt Extracts: Cause for Caution," *Brewing Techniques* (July/August 1993): 25–28.

4. Carol O'Neil, "Extract Magic," *Zymurgy* 17, no. 5 (Winter 1994): 34–41.

5. Suzanne Berens, "Brewing a Pale Beer With Extract," *Brew Your Own* (May 1997): 21–22.

6. Daniels, *Designing Great Beers*, 11.

7. Fix and Fix, *An Analysis of Brewing Techniques*, 24–30.

8. Ibid., 28–29.

9. Ibid., 7–10.

10. Daniels, *Designing Great Beers*, 40–62.

11. Neil C. Gudmestad and Raymond J. Taylor, "Malt: A Spectrum of Colors and Flavors," *Zymurgy* (Special Issue 1995): 11–12; "Lot Analyses: Technical Specifications," *The 1997 Brewers Market Guide* (Eugene, Ore.: New Wine Press, 1997): 100–104.

12. Trevor Wainwright, "Using sugar adjuncts in brewing," *Brewer's Guardian* (December 1993): 16–17.

13. Jeff Frane, "How Sweet It Is: Brewing with Sugar," *Zymurgy* 17, no. 1 (Spring 1994): 38–41.

14. Jean De Clerck, *A Textbook of Brewing* (London: Chapman and Hall, 1957), 319; Fix and Fix, *An Analysis of Brewing Techniques*, 45.

15. Fix and Fix, *An Analysis of Brewing Techniques*, 35–37.

16. Haydon, "The Beauty of Hops," *American Brewer* (Summer 1996): 44–47.

17. Mark Garetz, *Using Hops* (Danville, Calif.: HopTech, 1994), 36.

18. Nickerson and L. Van Engel, "Hop Aroma Component Profile and the Aroma Unit," *Journal of the American Society of Brewing Chemists* 50 (1992): 77.

19. Stephen Beaumont, "Single Hop Varietal Beers," *All About Beer* (May 1998): 15–17.
20. Garetz, *Using Hops*, 88–89.
21. Tim Kostelecky and David Hysert, "The Hop Shop," *Zymurgy* 20, no. 4 (Special Issue 1997): 33–34.
22. *Laboratory Methods for Craft Brewers* (St. Paul, Minn.: The American Society of Brewing Chemists, 1997), 41–45.
23. Amahl Turczyn, "The Mystery of First-Wort Hopping," *Zymurgy* (Special Issue 1997): 74.
24. Gerald Reed and Tilak W. Nagodawithana, *Yeast Technology* (New York: Van Nostrand Reinhold, 1991), 91.
25. Fix and Fix, *An Analysis of Brewing Techniques*, 56–65.
26. Ibid., 63.
27. Ibid., 75–81; Karl King, "Yeast Culturing Practices for Small-Scale Brewers," *Brewing Techniques* (May/June 1994): 37–41; Fal Allen, "The Microbrewery Laboratory Manual, Part I: Yeast Management," *Brewing Techniques* (July/August 1994): 28–35.
28. Fix and Fix, *An Analysis of Brewing Techniques*, 84–95.
29. Ibid., 18–20; Daniels, *Designing Great Beers*, 66.
30. Fix and Fix, *An Analysis of Brewing Techniques*, 21–22.

Chapter 4: Packaging and Dispensing Methods

1. Erin O'Connor-Cox, "Improving yeast handling in the brewery," *Brewer's Guardian* (March 1998): 20.
2. Michael Jackson, "In search of the bright beer secret," *Brewer's Guardian* (July 1996): 15.

3. Taylor, "The Fining of Cask Beer," *The Brewer* (May 1993): 202–205.

4. J. Scott Cowper and Robert Taylor, "Making Things Clear," *MBAA Technical Quarterly*, 25 (1988): 90–93.

5. Christine Fleming, "Fine Principles," *Small Beer* (March 1996): 7–8.

6. "Dissolved Carbon Dioxide," *Laboratory Methods of Craft Brewers* (St. Paul, Minn.: The American Society of Brewing Chemists, 1997): 38; Cliff Tanner, "Gas Gossip," *Zymurgy* (Summer 1994): 54; Ed Westemeier, "A Bottler's Guide to Kegging," *Zymurgy* (Summer 1995): 50; Kirk R. Fleming, "Discover the Joys of Kegging," *Brewing Techniques* (January/February 1997): 27.

7. Jeff Evans, *The CAMRA Guide to Real Ale in a Bottle* (St. Albans, England: CAMRA Books, 1997).

8. Tim O'Rourke, "Producing live ale in a bottle," *Small Beer* (March 1996): 18–19.

9. Fix and Fix, *An Analysis of Brewing Techniques*, 138–139.

10. Cliff Tanner, "Gas Gossip: Nitrogen vs. Carbon Dioxide Brewing," *Zymurgy* 17, no. 2 (Summer 1994): 52–56.

11. Fal Allen, "Laconic Technical Brewing Tips," *American Brewer*, no. 71 (Summer 1997): 74–76.

12. Peter Wesley, "Keeping and serving cask ale," *Brewers' Guardian* (June 1994): 15–20.

13. Ted Bruning, "Move to keep brewers up to Marque," *What's Brewing* (December 1997): 5.

14. Dick Cantwell, Fal Allen, and Kevin Forhan, "Beer from the Stainless," *Brewing Techniques* (November/December 1993): 22–28.

15. Ivor Clissold, *Cellarmanship* (St. Albans, England: CAMRA Books, 1997), 74–75.
16. Ray Daniels, "Beer from the Wood," *All About Beer* (July 1997): 16.
17. Ibid., 16.
18. Ibid., 15–16; Jason Dunson-Todd, "Beer from the Wood," *Brewing Techniques* (September 1997): 69.
19. Dunson-Todd, "Beer from the Wood," 65.
20. Fal Allen, "Beer Thrall," *American Brewer*, no. 77 (1998): 38–39.
21. Glen Falconer, "Real Ale at Home," *Zymurgy* 15, no. 4 (Special Issue 1992): 29.
22. Dunson-Todd, "Beer from the Wood," 62.
23. Sal Emma, "Build a Beer Engine," *Brew Your Own* (May 1997): 47–52.

Glossary

adjunct. 1. Any unmalted grain or other fermentable ingredient added to the mash. 2. A source of fermentable extract other than malted barley. Principally corn, rice, wheat, unmalted barley, and glucose (dextrose).

aerate. To force atmospheric air or oxygen into solution. To introduce air to the wort at various stages of the brewing process.

aeration. The action of introducing air to the wort at various stages of the brewing process.

aerobic. In the presence of or requiring oxygen.

airlock. *See* fermentation lock.

alcohol by volume (ABV). The percentage of volume of alcohol per volume of beer. To calculate the approximate volumetric alcohol content, subtract the final gravity from the original gravity and divide the result by 75. For example: 1.050 − 1.012 = 0.038 / 0.0075 = 5% ABV.

alcohol by weight (ABW). The percentage weight of alcohol per volume of beer. For example, 3.2% alcohol by weight = 3.2 grams of alcohol per 100 centiliters of beer. Alcohol by weight can be converted to alcohol by volume by multiplying by 0.795.

ale. 1. Historically, an unhopped malt beverage. 2. Now, a generic term for hopped beers produced by top fermentation, as opposed to lagers, which are produced by bottom fermentation.

all-extract beer. A beer made with only malt extract as opposed to one made from barley or a combination of malt extract and barley.

all-grain beer. A beer made with only malted barley as opposed to one made from malt extract or from malt extract and malted barley.

alpha acid unit (AAU). The number of AAUs in a hop addition is equal to the weight of the addition in ounces times the alpha acid percentage. Thus, 1 ounce of 5% alpha acid hops contain 5 AAUs. AAU is the same as homebrewers bittering units (HBU).

alpha acid (a-acid). The principal source of bitterness from hops when isomerized by boiling. These separate but related alpha acids come from the soft alpha resin of the hop. (When boiled, alpha acids are converted to iso-alpha-acids.)

ambient temperature. The surrounding temperature.

anaerobic. Conditions under which there is not enough oxygen for respiratory metabolic function. Anaerobic microorganisms are those that can function without the presence of free molecular oxygen.

apparent attenuation. A simple measure of the extent of fermentation that a wort has undergone in the process of becoming beer. When gravity units (GU), Balling (B) units, or Plato (P) units are used to express gravity, apparent attenuation is equal to the original gravity (OG) minus the terminal gravity divided by the OG. The result is expressed as a percentage and equals 65 to 80% for most beers.

apparent extract. The terminal gravity of a beer.

aqueous. Of water.

attemperate. To regulate or modify the temperature.

attenuate. To reduce the extract/density by yeast metabolism.

attenuation. The reduction in the wort's specific gravity caused by the transformation of sugars into ethanol and carbon dioxide gas.

autolysis. Yeast death due to shock or nutrient-depleted solutions.

Balling. A saccharometer invented by Carl Joseph Napoleon Balling in 1843. A standard for the measurement of the density of solutions. It is calibrated for 63.5 °F (17.5 °C) and graduated in grams per 100, giving a direct reading of the percentage of extract by weight per 100 grams solution. For example, 10 degrees Balling (°B) 10 grams of cane sugar per 100 grams of solution.

beerstone. Brownish gray mineral-like deposits left on fermentation equipment. Composed of calcium oxalate and organic residues.

blow-by (blow-off). A single-stage homebrewing fermentation method in which a plastic tube is fitted into the mouth of a carboy, with its other end submerged in a pail of sterile water. Unwanted residues and carbon dioxide are expelled through the tube, while air is prevented from coming into contact with the fermenting beer, thus avoiding contamination.

body. A qualitative indicator of the fullness or mouthfeel of a beer. Related to the proportion of unfermentable long-chain sugars or dextrins present in the beer.

Brettanomyces. A genus of yeast that has a role in the production of some beers, such as modern *lambics*, Berliner *weisse*, and historical porters.

brewer's gravity (SG). *See* gravity.

BU:GU ratio. The ratio of bitterness units (BU) to gravity units (GU) for a specific beer or group of beers. International bitterness units (IBU) are used for bitterness, and gravity units (GU) are used for the gravity component. GU = original gravity – 1 × 1,000. For most beers and beer styles, the resulting ratio has a value between 0.3 and 1.0.

buffer. A substance capable of resisting changes in the pH of a solution.

carbonate. An alkaline salt whose anions are derived from carbonic acid.

carbonation. The process of introducing carbon dioxide gas into a liquid by (1) injecting the finished beer with carbon dioxide; (2) adding young fermenting beer to finished beer for a renewed fermentation (kraeusening); (3) priming (adding sugar or wort to) fermented wort prior to bottling, thereby creating a secondary fermentation in the bottle; or (4) finishing fermentation under pressure.

carboy. A large glass, plastic, or earthenware bottle.

chill haze. Haziness caused by protein and tannin during the secondary fermentation.

chill-proof. Cold conditioning to precipitate chill haze.

closed fermentation. Fermentation under closed, anaerobic conditions to minimize risk of contamination and oxidation.

colloid. A gelatinous substance in solution.

decoction. Boiling the part of the mash that is boiled.

density. The measurement of the weight of a solution, as compared to the weight of an equal volume of pure water.

dextrin. Soluble polysaccharide fraction from hydrolysis of starch by heat, acid, or enzyme.

diacetyl. *See* diketone.

diacetyl rest. A warm—55 to 70 °F (13 to 21 °C)—rest that occurs during fermentation. During the diacetyl rest, yeast metabolize diacetyl and other byproducts of fermentation.

diastase. Starch-reducing enzymes. Usually alpha- and beta-amylase, but also limit dextrinase and a-glucosidase (maltase).

diastatic malt extract. A type of malt extract containing the diastatic enzymes naturally found in malt and needed for conversion of starch into sugar. This type of extract is sometimes used in recipes that contain grain adjuncts such as corn or rice.

diketone. A class of aromatic, volatile compounds perceivable in minute concentrations, from yeast or *Pediococcus* bacteria metabolism—most significantly, the butter and butterscotch aroma of diacetyl, a vicinal diketone (VDK). The other significant compound relevant to brewing is 2,3-pentanedione.

disaccharide. Sugar group. Two monosaccharide molecules joined by the removal of a water molecule.

dry hopping. The addition of hops to the primary fermenter, the secondary fermenter, or casked beer to add aroma and hop character to the finished beer without adding significant bitterness.

dry malt. Malt extract in powdered form.

European Brewery Convention (EBC). *See* SRM.

enzyme. A protein-based organic catalyst that effects changes in the compositions of the substances on which they act.

essential oil. The aromatic volatile compounds from the hop.

esters. Compounds from fermentation composed of an acid and an alcohol, such as the "banana" ester. Formed by yeast enzymes from an alcohol and an acid. Associated with ale and high-temperature fermentations, esters also arise to some extent with pure lager yeast cultures, although more so with low wort oxygenation, high initial fermentation temperatures, and high-gravity wort. Top-fermenting yeast strains are prized for their ability to produce particular mixes of aromatic esters. Tends to have fruity aromas and be detectable at low concentrations.

extract. The amount of dissolved materials in the wort after mashing and lautering malted barley and/or malt adjuncts such as corn and rice.

extraction. Drawing out the soluble essence of the malt or hops.

fermentation lock. A one-way valve that allows carbon dioxide gas to escape from the fermenter while excluding contaminants.

final specific gravity. The specific gravity of a beer when fermentation is complete.

fining. (n.) A clarifying agent. (v.) The process of adding clarifying agents to beer during secondary fermentation to precipitate suspended matter. Examples of clarifying agents are isinglass, gelatin, and bentonite.

flocculation. The tendency of yeast to clump together at the end of fermentation. The greater the tendency for the yeast to flocculate, the faster it will drop out of the solution, thereby creating clearer or brighter beer.

gravity (SG). Specific gravity as expressed by brewers. Specific gravity 1.046 is expressed as 1046 Density of a solution as compared to water. Expressed in grams per milliliter (1 milliliter water weighs 1 gram, hence sp. gr. 1.000 = SG 1000; sp. gr. 1.046 = SG 1046).

gravity units (GU). A form of expressing specific gravity in formulas as a whole number. It is equal to the significant digits to the right of the decimal point (1.055 SG becomes 55 GU, and 1.108 SG becomes 108 GU).

green malt. Malt that has been steeped and germinated and is ready for kilning.

gruit. A mixture of spices and herbs used to bitter and flavor ales before the acceptance of hops as a bittering and flavoring agent.

homebrewers bittering units (HBU). A formula adopted by the American Homebrewers Association to measure bitterness of beer. Example: 1.5 ounces of hops at 10% alpha acid for 5 gallons: 1.5 × 10 = 15 HBU per 5 gallons. Same as alpha acid unit (AAU).

hop pellets. Hop cones compressed into tablets. Hop pellets are 20 to 30% more bitter by weight than the same hop variety in loose form. Hop pellets are less subject to alpha acid losses than are whole hops.

hydrolysis. Decomposition of matter into soluble fractions by either acids or enzymes in water.

hydrometer. A glass instrument used to measure the specific gravity of liquids as compared to water, consisting of a graduated stem resting on a weighted float.

hydroxide. A compound, usually alkaline, containing the OH (hydroxyl) group.

inoculate. The introduction of a microbe into surroundings capable of supporting its growth.

international bitterness unit (IBU). A standard unit that measures the concentration of iso-alpha-acids in milligrams per liter (parts per million). Most procedures will also measure a small amount of uncharacterized soft resins, so IBUs are generally 5 to 15% higher than iso-alpha-acid concentrations.

isinglass. A gelatinous substance made from the swim bladder of certain fish and added to beer as a fining agent.

isomer (ISO). Organic compounds of identical composition and molecular weight but having a different molecular structure.

kilning. The final stage in the malting of barley that prepares it for use by the brewer. Kilning reduces the moisture contained in the grain to approximately 4% and also roasts the malt to some extent. The degree of roasting affects the flavor and color of the malt as well as of the beer it produces.

kraeusen. (n.) The rocky head of foam that appears on the surface of the wort during fermentation. Also used to describe the period of fermentation characterized by a rich foam head. (v.) To add fermenting wort to fermented beer to induce carbonation through a secondary fermentation.

Lactobacillus. Species of bacteria that ferments wort sugars to produce lactic acid. Although considered undesirable in most breweries and beer styles, it plays a significant role in the production of some beers, such as Berliner *weisse* and *lambics*.

lactophilic. An organism that metabolizes lactate more readily than glucose.

lager. (n.) A generic term for any bottom-fermented beer. Lager brewing is now the predominant brewing method worldwide except in Britain, where top-fermented ales dominate. (v.) To store beer at near-freezing temperatures in order to precipitate yeast cells and proteins and improve taste.

lauter. The process of separating the clear liquid from the spent grain and husks.

lauter tun. A vessel in which the mash settles and the grains are removed from the sweet wort through a straining process. It has a false slotted bottom and spigot.

liquefaction. The process by which alpha-amylase enzymes degrade soluble starch into dextrin.

malt. Barley that has been steeped in water, germinated, and then dried in kilns. This process converts insoluble starches to soluble substances and sugars.

malt extract. A thick syrup or dry powder prepared from malt.

maltose. A disaccharide composed of two glucose molecules. The primary sugar obtained by diastatic hydrolysis of starch. One-third the sweetness of sucrose.

mashing. Mixing ground malt with water to extract the fermentables, degrade haze-forming proteins, and convert grain starches to fermentable sugars and nonfermentable carbohydrates.

melanoidin. A color-producing compound produced through a long series of chemical reactions that begin with the combination of a sugar and an amino acid.

modification. 1. The physical and chemical changes that occur in barley during malting, where complex molecules are broken down to simpler, soluble molecules. 2. The degree to which malt has undergone these changes, as determined by the growth of the acrospire. The greater the degree of modification, the more readily available starch is and the lower the protein level is.

original gravity (OG). The specific gravity of wort previous to fermentation. A measure of the total amount of dissolved solids in wort.

oxidation. 1. The combining of oxygen with other molecules, often causing off-flavors, as with oxidized alcohols, to form aldehydes. 2. A reaction in which the atoms in an element lose electrons and the element's valence is correspondingly increased (oxidation-reduction reaction).

parti-gyle. An arcane system of brewing in which the first runnings of wort are taken to make a high-gravity beer and the grain is then remashed to create another brew. This can be done yet again to make a third brew, all from the same grains. There is usually no sparging involved. With the advent of more sophisticated equipment that allowed lautering and sparging, the parti-gyle system of brewing lost favor around the end of the nineteenth century.

pH. A measure of acidity or alkalinity of a solution, on a scale of 1 to 14, where 7 is neutral.

phosphate. A salt or ester of phosphoric acid.

pitching. Inoculating sterile wort with a vigorous yeast culture.

Plato, degrees. Commercial brewers' standard for the measurement of the density of solutions, expressed as the equivalent weight of cane sugar in solution (calibrated on grams of sucrose per 100 grams of solution). Like degrees Balling, but Plato's computations are more exact.

Plato saccharometer. A saccharometer that expresses specific gravity as extract weight in a 100-gram solution at 68 °F (20 °C). A revised, more accurate version of Balling, developed by Dr. Plato.

polymer. A compound molecule formed by the joining of many smaller identical units. For example, polyphenols from phenols and polypeptides from peptides.

polysaccharide. A carbohydrate complex, able to be reduced to monosaccharides by hydrolysis.

ppm. Parts per million. Equal to milligrams per liter (mg/l). The measurement of particles of matter in solution.

precipitation. Separation of suspended matter by sedimentation.

precursor. The starting materials or inputs for a chemical reaction.

primary fermentation. The first stage of fermentation, during which most fermentable sugars are converted to ethyl alcohol and carbon dioxide.

priming. The act of adding priming sugar to a still (or flat) beer so that it can develop carbonation.

priming solution. A solution of sugar in water added to aged beer at bottling to induce fermentation (bottle conditioning).

priming sugar. A small amount of corn, malt, or cane sugar added to bulk beer prior to racking or at bottling to induce a new fermentation and to create carbonation.

protein. A generally amorphous and colloidal complex amino acid containing about 16% nitrogen with carbon, hydrogen, oxygen, and possibly sulfur, phosphorous, and iron. True protein has a molecular weight of 17,000 to 150,000+. In beer, protein will have been largely decomposed to a molecular weight of 5,000 to 12,000 (albumin or proteoses), 400 to 1,500 (peptides), or amino acids. Protein as a haze fraction ranges from molecular weight 10,000 to 100,000 (average 30,000) and as the stabilizing component of foam, from 12,000 to 20,000.

proteolysis. The reduction of protein by proteolytic enzymes to fractions.

racking. The process of transferring beer from one container to another, especially into the final package (bottles, kegs, and so on).

reagent. A substance involved in a reaction that identifies the strength of the substance being measured.

real ale. A style of beer found primarily in England, where it has been championed by the consumer rights group called the Campaign for Real Ale (CAMRA). Generally defined as a beer that has undergone a secondary fermentation in the container from which it is served and that is served without the application of carbon dioxide.

resin. Noncrystalline (amorphous) plant excretion.

rest. Mash rest. Holding the mash at a specific temperature to induce certain enzymatic changes.

rousing. Creating turbulence by agitation. Mixing.

runnings. The wort or sweet liquid that is collected during the lautering of the wet mash.

saccharification. The naturally occurring process in which malt starch is converted into fermentable sugars, primarily maltose. Also called mashing, since saccharification occurs during the mash rest.

saccharometer. An instrument that determines the sugar concentration of a solution by measuring the specific gravity.

secondary fermentation. 1. The second, slower stage of fermentation, which, depending on the type of beer, lasts from a few weeks to many months. 2. A fermentation occurring in bottles or casks and initiated by priming or by adding yeast.

sparge. The even distribution or spray of hot water over the saccharified mash to rinse free the extract from the grist.

sparging. Spraying the spent grains in the mash with hot water to retrieve the remaining malt sugar. This is done at the end of the mashing (saccharification) process.

specific gravity (SG). A measure of a substance's density as compared to that of water, which is given the value of 1.000 at 39.2 °F (4 °C). Specific gravity has no accompanying units because it is expressed as a ratio. Specific gravity is the density of a solution in grams per milliliter.

Standard Reference Method (SRM) and **European Brewery Convention (EBC).** Two different analytical methods of describing color developed by comparing color samples. Degrees SRM, approximately equivalent to degrees Lovibond, are used by the

ASBC (American Society of Brewing Chemists), while degrees EBC are European units. The following equations show approximate conversions: (EBC) = 2.65 × (SRM) − 1.2; SRM = 0.377 × (EBC) + 0.46.

starch. A polymer of sugar molecules. The chief form of energy storage for most plants. It is from starch that the relevant sugars for brewing are derived.

starter. A batch of fermenting yeast added to the wort to initiate fermentation.

strike temperature. The initial (target) temperature of the water when the malted barley is added to it to create the mash.

tannin. Astringent polyphenolic compound, capable of colliding with proteins and either precipitating or forming haze fractions. Oxidized polyphenols form color compounds relevant in beer. *See also* polyphenol.

terminal extract. The density of the fully fermented beer.

trub. Flocks of haze-forming particles resulting from the precipitation of proteins, hop oils, and tannins during the boiling and cooling stages of brewing.

turbidity. Sediment in suspension. Hazy, murky.

ullage. The empty space between a liquid and the top of its container. Also called airspace or headspace.

viscosity. The resistance of a fluid to flow.

volatile. Readily vaporized. Applies especially to esters, essential oils, and higher alcohols.

volume of beer. To calculate the approximate volumetric alcohol content, subtract the terminal gravity from the original gravity and divide the result by 75. For example: $1.050 - 1.012 = 0.038 / 0.75 = 0.05$ or 5% ABV.

water hardness. The degree of dissolved minerals in water. Usually expressed in parts per million (ppm) or grains per gallon (gpg).

wort. Mash extract (sweet wort). The hopped sugar solution before pitching, before it is fermented into beer.

Index

Index

326

Index

Busch, Jim: on choosing hops, 171

Caffreys bitter, 31

Cain's, bitters from, 280

Calcium carbonate, 200, 205; adding, 202, 203

California Steam Beer, 122

Calverley, Charles Stuart, 15

Campaign for Real Ale (CAMRA), 1, 227; bottle-conditioned beers and, 222; carbon dioxide and, 94; on casks, 234; protest by, 71, 77–78; real ale and, 81; serving and, 226

CAMRA Beer Guide 1997 (CAMRA Books), 275, 276

CAMRA Guide to Real Ale in a Bottle (Evans), 275

Cane sugar, 163, 221; fermentability and, 161; priming with, 220

Caramelization, 153, 160, 248

Caramel malts, 93, 153–57; function of, 137; producing, 153–54

Carbonate, 202, 312; removing, 200, 201

Carbonation, 312; artificial, 226, 227; determining amount of, 220 (table); forced, 133; kegs and, 224; purpose of, 217–21

Carbonation stone, 219

Carbon dioxide, 75, 104, 133, 226, 227, 229; adding, 218, 219; level of, 74; measuring, 218; real ale and, 94, 233

Carboys, 312; inversion of, 188; yeast and, 187

Carlsberg-Tetley, Bass and, 78–79

Carlton United Breweries, 73

Carrageenan, 211, 216

Cascade hops, 172, 270, 274; flavor of, 128; using, 88, 89, 90, 91, 121, 169, 173, 205

Cask breathers, 233, 234

Cask conditioning, 74, 75, 94, 102, 104, 109, 110, 113, 123, 210, 223, 227, 228–34; dry hopping and, 111, 181–82; fining and, 208; hops and, 181; isinglass and, 214; secondary fermentation during, 228; sugar priming and, 135; yeast in, 192

Cask Marque, 232

Casks, 209, 215, 229–30; coopered, 235; cost of, 240–41; equipment for, 241; oak, 87, 235–36; stainless steel, 234–35, 235 (photo), 236, 239–42, 240 (photo); steam cleaning, 86; suppliers of, 245; treating, 87, 239; wooden, 87, 132, 234, 235, 235 (photo), 239–42

Castlemaine XXXX, 73

Catamount Amber Ale, 92, 282

Catamount Brewing Company, 122 (photo)

Cathedral Bitter, 278

Cellars, temperature in, 231, 232

Cereal cooker, 162

Cereals, 62, 160, 161

Character, 101, 102; fermentation and, 185; malt, 140, 157; oaky, 236, 237. *See also* Hop character; Malt character

Charles II, taxation by, 59

Charrington, 39

Cheriton Brewhouse, 167 (photo); bitter from, 277

Chill haze, 61, 74, 160, 213, 217, 313; problems with, 145, 161

Chloramines, 200

Chlorine, removing, 200

Christmas ales, 11

Clarification, 196, 225; finings and, 211–17; Irish moss and, 212

Co-humulone, 168

Coke, using, 12–14

Collagen, 212, 214

Color, 68, 69, 125; bittering and, 111; malts and, 142, 155–56; style and, 112

Commercial brewers, 34, 82; pub buying spree by, 35; style definitions and, 101

Commonwealth Brewery, 282

Index

Index

Index

Index

Index

Index

About the Author

A Londoner—born, bred, and educated—Terry Foster has lived in Connecticut for the last 20 years. He is fluent in both English and American and will sometimes use both in the same sentence—usually when led astray by someone forcing beer upon him. He holds a Ph.D. in chemistry from the University of London. He currently is an Associate Research Fellow for the world's major producer of mineral processing chemicals. More specifically, he runs the global technical service function of the company in the application of water-soluble polymers to the processing of bauxite into alumina, the precursor of aluminum. It is a job that requires a good deal of travel around the world and forces him to taste locally produced beers in some unlikely places. Normally an upstanding citizen, he did once get arrested in Poland for having parked under a no parking sign in front of a police station while heading to the local pub.

Foster has been brewing for almost 40 years and isn't tired of doing so. Indeed, he finds one of the worst parts of his job is that the traveling interferes with his brewing. He was privileged to have been present at the renaissance of homebrewing in both England and America—although the memory of those early days sometimes keeps him awake at night, wondering about the poor quality of the ingredients he was occasionally forced to use. He has written extensively on many aspects of brewing in virtually all of the major brewing and beer magazines in England and in America. He also can occasionally be persuaded to give talks on the subject to interested groups. His first book, *Dr. Foster's Book of Beer*, was published in England in 1978. This was followed by *Pale Ale*, the first in Brewers Publications' Classic Beer Style Series, and later by *Porter* in the same series.

He loves Young's Special, Fuller's London Pride, Timothy Taylor's Landlord, and Anchor Liberty Ale—and New England seafood, especially lobster. He used to like the Red Sox, until baseball prostituted itself to money and he could no longer tell from day to day which players were on which team! He hates both the name and lack of taste of "lite" beers and has been known to stay completely sober at parties where the host served only industrial beers. He thinks life is far too short to waste time on drinking bland beer.